Mastery of Your Anxiety and Panic

Second Edition

Client Workbook

David H. Barlow
Michelle G. Craske

Copyright © 1994 by Graywind Publications Incorporated

All rights reserved. No part of this publication may be reproduced or transmitted in any form or by any means, electronic or mechanical, including photocopy, recording, or any information storage and retrieval system, without permission in writing from the publisher.

The Psychological Corporation and the *PSI* logo are registered trademarks of The Psychological Corporation.

TherapyWorks is a registered trademark of The Psychological Corporation.

The TherapyWorks series is a Graywind publication and a product of The Psychological Corporation.

Printed in the United States of America

2 3 4 5 6 7 8 9 10 11 12 A B C D E

Contents

Chapter 1: Controlled by or Control Over Your Emotions 1
    What Are Panic and Anxiety: Is This Program Right for You? 1
    Do You Have Panic Disorder or Agoraphobia? 3
    How Common Is This Problem? 5
    How Are You Coping With Your Panic Attacks Now? 6
        Avoidance 6
        Distraction 7
        Superstitious Coping Methods 7
        Alcohol and Other Drugs 8
    Other Disorders 8
    What Causes Panic and Anxiety? 9
    Do You Fit This Program? 10
    Alternative Treatments 11
    Are You Taking Drugs for Your Anxiety? 11
    What Benefits Will You Receive From This Program? 12
    What Costs Will You Pay? 12
    Brief Description of the Program 13
    Self-Assessment 16

Chapter 2: Learning About Your Reactions 17
    Why Should You Learn to Be an Observer? 17
    What to Monitor 18
        Panic Attacks 18
        Anxiety 21
        Progress 23
        Activities and Places 23
    Summary 23
    Exercise 25
    Self-Assessment 25

Chapter 3: Developing a Perspective for Changing Your Reactions 27
    Review 27
    What Is Anxiety? 28
    How Does It All Begin? 33
    Training Program Rationale 36

	Exercise	37
	Self-Assessment	38
Chapter 4:	**What Produces the Panic Feelings**	39
	Review	39
	The Physiology of Panic	39
	Nervous and Chemical Effects	40
	Cardiovascular Effects	41
	Respiratory Effects	42
	Sweat Gland Effects	42
	Other Physical Effects	42
	The Behavior of Panic	43
	The Thoughts of Panic	43
	But How Does Panic Occur?	44
	Common Myths	49
	Going Crazy	49
	Losing Control	49
	Nervous Collapse	51
	Heart Attacks	51
	Fainting	52
	Summary	52
	Exercise	53
	Self-Assessment	53
Chapter 5:	**Learning Physical Control**	55
	Review	55
	Control of Physical Sensations	55
	Breathing Physiology	57
	Breathing Control Procedures	59
	The First Breathing Control Exercise	59
	Muscle Relaxation Training	63
	Exercises	71
	Self-Assessment	71
Chapter 6:	**Development of Control of Physical Responses**	73
	Review	73
	Breathing Control	73
	Muscle Relaxation	74
	Exercise	75
	Self-Assessment	76

Chapter 7: **Refinement of Physical Response Control Techniques and an Introduction to Self-Statement Analysis** 77
    Review 77
    Breathing Control 77
    Relaxation Training 78
    Beginning of Self-Statement Analysis 79
    Identifying Probability Overestimation 82
    Challenging Probability Overestimation 85
    Exercise 90
    Self-Assessment 90

Chapter 8: **Continuation of Self-Statement Analysis Manipulating Your Own Mind** 91
    Review 91
    Breathing Retraining 91
    Relaxation Training 92
    Catastrophic Thinking 92
    Exercise 98
    Self-Assessment 100

Chapter 9: **The Unexpected Becomes Predictable** 101
    Review 101
    Breathing Control and Relaxation Training 101
    Self-Statements 101
    Prediction Testing 102
    Looking for Causes of Unexpected Panics 104
        Physical State 106
        Thoughts 107
        General Stressors 107
    Exercise 107
    Self-Assessment 107

Chapter 10: **Producing the Panic Sensations** 109
    Review 109
    Response Component Strategies 109
    Repeated Practice With Panic Sensations—Why? 110
    Identifying Which Sensations Are Fearful 111
    Repeated Practice With Bodily Sensations 117
    Exercise 121
    Self-Assessment 122

Chapter 11: Producing Panic Sensations in Your Daily Life 123
Review 123
Continued Exposure Exercise 123
Activities Exposure 124
What to Do if Anxiety and Panic Recur 125
Exercise 127
Self-Assessment 127

Chapter 12: Producing Panic Sensations in Your Daily Life—Continued 129
Review 129
Confrontation With Fear in Your Daily Life—General Issues 129
Confrontation With Fear in Your Daily Life—Specifics 132
Dealing With Frightening Memories 133
Exercise 136
Self-Assessment 137

Chapter 13: Overcoming Your Phobic Avoidance: Producing Panic Sensations in Agoraphobic Situations 139
Review 139
Conquering Agoraphobia—Back to the Shopping Mall 141
Summary of Steps for Overcoming Agoraphobic Avoidance 142
Exercise 145
Self-Assessment 145

Chapter 14: Medication Issues 147
Review 147
Medications in the Treatment of Panic and Anxiety 147
Low-Potency Benzodiazepines (Minor Tranquilizers) 148
High-Potency Benzodiazepines 149
Antidepressants 149
Beta Blockers 150
Stopping Your Medication 151
Exercise 152
Self-Assessment 152

Chapter 15: Your Accomplishments and Your Future 155
Self-Evaluation 155
What to Do Next 157
Maintenance Planning 158
High-Risk Times 159

Appendix A: Answers for Self-Assessment Questions 161

References 173

Figures

Figure 1.1. Decision Tree 14
Figure 2.1. Jill's First Panic Attack Record 20
Figure 2.2. Jill's Second Panic Attack Record 20
Figure 2.3. Jill's Daily Mood Record 22
Figure 2.4. Progress Record 24
Figure 3.1. A Completed Anxiety Components Form 30
Figure 3.2. A Completed Panic Components Form 31
Figure 3.3. A Completed Panic Sequences Form 34
Figure 4.1. The Cycle of a Panic Attack 47
Figure 5.1. Example of Breathing Retraining Record 62
Figure 5.2. Example of Relaxation Record Form 69
Figure 7.1. Example of Modifying Self-Statement—Overestimations Form 89
Figure 8.1. Example of Modifying Self-Statements II—Catastrophizing Form . . 97
Figure 8.2. Example of Self-Statement Rating Form 99
Figure 9.1. Example of Prediction Testing Form 103
Figure 10.1. Example of Sensation Induction Record 114
Figure 10.2. Example (Partial) of Exposure Exercise Record 120
Figure 12.1. Example of Activities Hierarchy Form 130
Figure 12.2. Example of Exposure Exercise Record Form 134
Figure 13.1. Example of Agoraphobic-Avoided Situations 143
Figure 15.1. Self-Evaluation Form 156

Comments About the Program

"Drs. Barlow and Craske have written an outstanding teaching module to be used by patients who suffer from panic, agoraphobia, and related anxiety states. The manual will be an invaluable addition to standard clinical treatment and a godsend to patients who live in areas where such treatment is not available."

> Ms. Katherine Shear, MD
> Director, Anxiety Disorders Clinic
> Payne Whitney Clinic
> Cornell University Medical College

"This method of treating panic attacks is clearly the best conceived and most useful approach yet devised. Dr. Barlow and Dr. Craske have made an important and effective advance in anxiety treatment."

> Jack M. Gorman, MD
> Chief, Department of Clinical Psychobiology
> New York State Psychiatric Institute and
> College of Physicians and Surgeons,
> Columbia University

"Drs. Barlow and Craske's manual is a great step forward in helping patients to gain control over panic attacks. It is simply the best of its kind."

> Scott Woods, MD
> Director, Anxiety Disorders Clinic
> Yale University Medical School

About the Authors

David H. Barlow received his PhD from the University of Vermont in 1969, and has published over 200 articles and chapters and 15 books, mostly in the areas of anxiety disorders, sexual problems, and clinical research methodology. Recent books *Clinical Handbook of Psychological Disorders: A Step-by-Step Treatment Manual* (2nd ed., 1993); *Anxiety and Its Disorders: The Nature and Treatment of Anxiety and Panic* (1988); and the revised guide to this book, *Therapist's Guide for the Mastery of Your Anxiety and Panic—Second Edition*, with M. G. Craske (1994).

Dr. Barlow was formerly professor of psychiatry and psychology at Brown University and Distinguished Professor in the Department of Psychology at the University at Albany–State University of New York. Currently he is professor of psychology, director of the Clinical Training Program, and director of the Center for Anxiety and Related Disorders at Boston University. Dr. Barlow is also past president of the Division of Clinical Psychology of the American Psychological Association. He has been a consultant to the National Institute of Mental Health (NIMH) and the National Institutes of Health since 1973 and was recently awarded a merit award from the NIMH for "research competence and productivity that are distinctly superior." He was a member of the DSM–IV Task Force. The major objective of his work for the last 15 years has been the development of new treatments for anxiety disorders.

Michelle G. Craske received her PhD from the University of British Columbia in 1985, and has published many articles and chapters in the area of anxiety disorders. Currently, she is associate professor in the Department of Psychology at the University of California, Los Angeles, and Director of the Anxiety Disorders Behavioral Program within the UCLA Psychology Clinic. Her research has focused on the development of specific treatments for anxiety, panic, and avoidance restrictions, and on variables of etiological and maintaining significance for patterns of fear and avoidance. She was a member of the DSM–IV Anxiety Disorders Workgroup Subcommittee for revision of the diagnostic criteria surrounding Panic Disorder and Simple Phobia.

Preface

This revision of *Mastery of Your Anxiety and Panic* program (MAP–II) updates and improves the previous program in numerous ways. The entire text has been rewritten to make it easier to read and more accessible to the consumer. Additionally, new methods for providing exposure to feared sensations have been incorporated into the new Workbook. Finally, a separate workbook titled the *Agoraphobia Supplement to the MAP–II Program* has been written to help clients for whom avoidance of fearful situations is also a problem.

We wish to acknowledge with deep appreciation the contribution of all present and former students and staff of the Center for Stress and Anxiety Disorders to the development of this treatment program. In particular, Jerry Cerny, PhD, and Janet Klosko, PhD, made invaluable contributions to our earlier version of this protocol. Ron Rapee, PhD, made a substantial contribution to the program and should be considered one of the originators. Finally, David A. Spiegel, MD, contributed substantially and effectively to Chapter 14 on medication issues.

We would also like to acknowledge that two of "The Far Side" cartoons by Gary Larson are reprinted by permission of Chronicle Features, San Francisco, California. Permission was also granted to reprint several of Gary Larson's cartoons by the Universal Press Syndicate, all rights reserved.

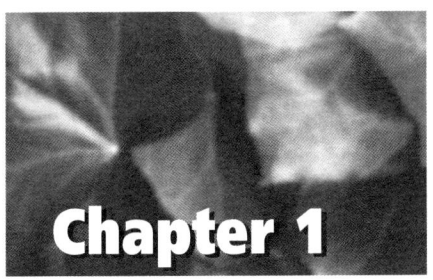

Chapter 1

Controlled by or Control Over Your Emotions

What Are Panic and Anxiety: Is This Program Right for You?

Do you feel at the mercy of your own emotions? Do you have repeated abrupt surges of intense fear or dread that make you think you are sick, dying, or losing your mind? When these scary attacks occur, does your heart feel as though it's going to burst out of your chest? Do you feel dizzy, faint, trembly, sweaty, short of breath, and scared to death? Do the scary feelings sometimes seem to come from "out of the blue," such as while at home relaxing? Does it feel as if you are "on guard", waiting for these feelings to happen again, so that you are constantly on edge, even when doing things that you used to find relaxing? Do you find yourself paying very close attention to different aspects of your bodily functions, such as your breathing or blood pressure, because any slight change may suggest the scary feelings are coming on again? Has your anticipation of the scary feelings interfered with your normal daily routine or prevented you from doing things you would normally do? This might include avoiding activities that bring on the feelings, such as drinking coffee. When you get into a car or go into a crowded store, are you worried about what to do should the feelings occur, how they might be tolerated, or how you can escape if necessary? Maybe the anticipation is so overwhelming that you try to avoid driving, crowded stores, or other situations where you feel trapped or where it seems difficult to get help. And, finally, do you think the scary feelings are going to cause you to die, faint, collapse, go crazy or be embarrassed?

Does this picture come close to describing you? If so, chances are you are having panic attacks and associated anxiety. Of course, there are many differences in the way in which people experience panic and anxiety. If you experience something like what was just described, then it is likely that the program in this Workbook will be helpful for you, as it has been for many people who have come to our clinic. One such person we will call Steve.

At the time, Steve was a 35-year-old, single sales manager who suffered episodes of dizziness, blurred vision, heart palpitations, and loss of concentration. The first episode occurred at work, in the presence of his coworkers, and began with feelings of weakness, nausea, and dizziness. He thought he was going to faint and asked a colleague to call a doctor. It seemed to him at the time that he could be suffering a stroke. His father had recently died of a heart attack. In addition, Steve was dealing with a lot of stress at work.

Several months before that first episode, Steve had had times when he was nervous and his writing had become shaky, but, apart from that, he had never experienced anything like this before. After a thorough physical exam, his doctor told him that it was stress and anxiety and referred him to our Anxiety Disorders Clinic. By the time he came to our clinic, the panics were occurring mostly at work, when driving, in restaurants, and at home. They were often unexpected, particularly the times that he woke from sleep in a panic. Between the panic episodes, Steve felt a great deal of tension and anxiety. He reported general symptoms such as jumpiness; restlessness; difficulty relaxing, sleeping, and concentrating; muscle twitching; pressure feelings around his chest; and a loss of confidence in himself. Since his third panic attack, Steve had begun to avoid being alone whenever possible, because he was afraid he could be in real danger if a severe attack occurred. He also avoided situations such as stores, malls, crowds, theaters, and lines, where he feared being trapped and embarrassed if he panicked. When he did have an attack, Steve would usually escape from the situation or ask for help. Wherever he went Steve carried a Bible, as well as gum and cigarettes, because glancing at the Bible or chewing gum or smoking cigarettes would make him feel more comfortable and better able to cope.

Susan was another person who benefited greatly from the kind of program described in this Workbook. She was 24 years old and single. She was having repeated attacks of dizziness, breathlessness, palpitations, chest pain, blurred vision, a lump in her throat, and a feeling of unreality, accompanied by a feeling of impending doom. She was afraid that she was going to have a heart attack or just lose control. The problem began around 2 years earlier following one of her first experiences with marijuana. While at a party, Susan smoked marijuana and, within a short while, began to feel very unreal and dizzy. Never having had these feelings before, Susan thought she was very ill and was afraid she was no longer in control. She asked a friend to take her to the emergency room. The physicians did some tests and reassured Susan that her symptoms were due to becoming anxious and hyperventilating. Susan never touched marijuana or other drugs after that. In fact, she became nervous about any chemical substances, even those prescribed for allergies and colds. Susan had gone back to the emergency room at least twice since the first time, both as a result of panicking. The attacks varied over the years in both intensity and frequency. At one point, she had no attacks for 3 months. However, she still worried most of the time about having another attack. She felt uneasy in situations where she thought she would be trapped if an attack occurred, but she did not actually avoid many places. She took alprazolam (Xanax®) to help her cope with her panics.

If you have had these kinds of feelings in the past and are currently not fearful, but would like to have some information that might be helpful in the event of a return of your fear, this Workbook should be worthwhile. However, this Workbook is designed primarily for those who are currently experiencing panic attacks or who are anxious or worried about panicking.

Do You Have Panic Disorder or Agoraphobia?

The classification system in use within the United States, and in many other countries is referred to as the *Diagnostic and Statistical Manual of Mental Disorders—Fourth Edition* (DSM–IV), published by the American Psychiatric Association (1994). It identifies the problem that this Workbook addresses as panic disorder with or without agoraphobia. The key features of this disorder are (a) one or more episodes of abrupt, intense fear or discomfort, that is, a panic attack, such as those experienced by Steve and Susan; and (b) persistent apprehension or worry about the recurrence of the episodes of intense fear or discomfort. The reason for the second component will become clearer later. In brief, occasional panic attacks are common, but not everyone who experiences panic attacks suffers from panic disorder.

Worrying about the possibility that you might have another panic attack seems to be the worst part, and it is a defining feature of the disorder. It is important to note that panic attacks are experienced by people with a variety of different anxiety problems. It is also important to remember the distinction between a panic attack and anxiety. A panic attack is a sudden or abrupt surge of fear that peaks quickly and then subsides within 10–30 minutes, although you may continue to feel some of the symptoms for a while afterwards. In contrast, anxiety tends to build more slowly and to be more generalized. The MAP–II program is designed for people who have the kind of panic attacks that become the major focus of worry and dread.

Another criterion of panic disorder according to the DSM–IV, at least one of the panic episodes must be unexpected and not caused by situations in which the individual is the focus of attention, such as giving a speech. The attacks are accompanied by physical symptoms such as those presented on the following page. Fears of going crazy, of dying, or of losing control also accompany these attacks.

Typical Panic Attack Symptoms

1. Difficulty breathing
2. Sweating
3. Chest pain or discomfort
4. Unsteadiness, dizziness, or faintness
5. Feelings of unreality or detachment
6. Trembling or shaking
7. Tingling or numbness
8. Nausea or abdominal distress
9. Palpitations or tachycardia
10. Choking or smothering sensations
11. Hot flashes or cold chills
12. Fear of dying
13. Fear of going crazy or losing control

Panic attacks are sometimes accompanied by avoidance of certain situations, places, or activities. Typically, these places or situations are those from which escape might be difficult or in which help might be unavailable. A common example is a crowded shopping mall, where it might be hard to find the exit and difficult to get through all the people, if he or she felt they had to leave suddenly because of a panic attack. Avoiding places or situations because of fear or panic, when no real danger exists, is called a *phobia*. Avoiding places or situations from which escape might be difficult or help unavailable in the event of a panic attack is called *agoraphobia*. This term is fitting because *agora* was the ancient Greek marketplace, or the original shopping mall. However, places and situations avoided by people with agoraphobia are not limited to malls. A partial list of agoraphobic situations is presented below.

Typical Agoraphobic Situations

1. Driving
2. Public transport—subways, buses, planes, taxis
3. Waiting in lines
4. Crowds
5. Stores
6. Restaurants
7. Theaters
8. Going a long distance from home
9. Long walks
10. Wide, open spaces
11. Closed-in spaces
12. Boats
13. Staying at home alone
14. Auditoriums
15. Elevators
16. Escalators

According to the diagnostic criteria for panic disorder, the episodes of panic cannot be the direct result of a physical problem, such as hyperthyroidism or excessive amphetamine or caffeine use (10 or more cups of coffee per day).

Although some physical problems can occur at the same time as a panic attack occurs and may even contribute to the likelihood of having an attack, these physical problems do not fully account for the attacks. Examples include hypoglycemia (low blood sugar) or mitral valve prolapse (a mild flutter of the heart). For example, it is possible for a person to have both mitral valve prolapse and panic disorder. Controlling the mitral valve prolapse symptoms does not necessarily eliminate the panic disorder, nor vice versa. Similarly, one may have times of feeling weak and shaky due to low blood-sugar levels, yet, even when the low blood sugar is corrected through diet, the panic attacks continue. Asthma, allergies, and gastrointestinal problems can also occur at the same time as a panic attack occurs.

We recommend to our clients who have not had a medical examination in the past year to have a full examination to check for possible physical causes of anxiety symptoms and to identify other physical factors that may contribute to panic and anxiety. These factors are then taken into account during the treatment program.

How Common Is This Problem?

Panic attacks and agoraphobia are very common. For example, the prevalence rate of agoraphobia is estimated to be 3%–6% of the general population. This means that in the United States alone, 7–12 million people have agoraphobia. In combination with other phobic and anxiety disorders, this rate increases to 10%–12%. This represents a larger proportion of the population than those with alcohol or other drug abuse problems and makes anxiety disorders the number one mental health problem in the United States. More attention has been devoted to panic disorder and agoraphobia recently, because we now know more about these disorders and can recognize them more readily in emergency rooms and doctors' offices.

In addition to those who have panic disorder and agoraphobia, many other people have just occasional panic attacks without developing panic disorder. For example, over 30% of the population has had some sort of panic attack during the past year, often in response to a very stressful situation such as an exam or giving a speech. Even when just counting panic attacks that seem to occur out of the blue, these are reported by 9%–14% of the population during the past year. Far fewer people develop a severe problem that needs treatment. This fact implies that most people who have panic attacks have ways of coping successfully with them. We discuss coping styles further in our discussion about ways to manage your own anxiety and panic.

The experience of panic and avoidance seems to occur across all kinds of people: across all levels of socioeconomic status, professions, and types of persons. The disorder also occurs in different cultures, although it may be labeled and understood differently, according to specific cultural beliefs. Recognition of panic disorder in other cultures has led to the translation of this Workbook into several other languages, including Chinese and Korean.

How Are You Coping With Your Panic Attacks Now?

We already mentioned a common way of coping with panic attacks: avoiding situations where they might occur. It is such a common method of coping that this phobic avoidance behavior has its own label: agoraphobia. But there are many other methods of coping with panic. Many of these methods help people get through a panic attack but do nothing to prevent future attacks. Furthermore, while some of the methods are not harmful, others can be extremely dangerous. The following sections describe the different methods of coping.

Avoidance

Avoidance refers to hesitating or refusing to enter certain situations, to take on certain tasks, or to engage in certain activities. It differs from escape, which is the act of leaving a situation, task or activity after having started it. Avoidance behavior is usually motivated by the expectation of something bad happening in the situation, task, or activity. Nevertheless, avoidance and escape are obviously closely related. We have already mentioned agoraphobic avoidance, but there are other types of avoidance that are more subtle, as the following examples show:

- Do you avoid drinking coffee?
- Do you avoid drinking alcohol?
- Do you avoid medication of any kind even if your doctor prescribes it?
- Do you avoid exercise?
- Do you avoid becoming very angry?
- Do you avoid sexual relations?
- Do you avoid watching horror movies or very sad movies?
- Do you avoid being outside in very hot or very cold conditions?
- Do you hate being startled or frightened?
- Do you avoid being away from medical help?

If yes, these forms of avoidance may well be connected to your panic attacks and should disappear when you successfully complete this program. The ways in which they are connected to panic attacks are described in the next couple of chapters.

Distraction

Many people attempt to "get through" situations in which they are worried about having a panic attack by distracting themselves. There is no limit to the ingenuity of methods that have been used as means of distraction. For example, if you feel yourself becoming anxious or panicky, do you:

- play loud music?
- carry around something to read such as the Bible, or some helpful coping statements, and read them as intensely as you can?
- pinch yourself?
- snap a rubber band on your wrist?
- place cold wet towels on your face?
- tell somebody who is with you to talk to you about something—anything?
- try to keep as busy as possible?
- keep the television on as you go to sleep?
- try to imagine yourself somewhere else?
- play counting games?
- think about caring for the persons with you—such as your children?

If you have tried any of these strategies, chances are they have helped you get through a panic attack in the past and may well help you in the future. However, these strategies often become strong habits that people come to depend on. For example, if you forget your reading material or your rubber band, you may have to go home to get it. Or you might just not go where you had planned to go because you do not have your distractor. In the long run, these strategies, although not harmful, are not helpful either because they do not alter the underlying processes that lead to panic attacks. Distraction is like placing tape around a broken table leg without fixing the break. As a result, distraction keeps the panic attacks and worry about having panic attacks alive and prevents corrective learning from taking place. More about this later.

Superstitious Coping Methods

Many people carry bottles of tranquilizers to take if they feel an anxiety or panic attack coming on. Medication taken under the supervision of a physician is okay, because your doctor will make sure you are using these drugs appropriately. However, taking such medication without a doctor's supervision is a dangerous practice. Some people use a less dangerous but superstitious habit. They carry around empty pill bottles in their purse or pocket. These people realize that nothing is in the bottles to help them if they have a panic attack. Nevertheless, they feel "better" and "safer" just having that bottle. This practice is an example of superstitious behavior. A list of superstitious safety objects used by some of our clients is presented on the following page.

Superstitious Safety Signals

1. Medication
2. Empty medication bottles
3. Food or drink
4. Smelling salts or antacid
5. Paper bags
6. Religious symbols
7. Objects such as flashlights, money, CB radios, cameras, bags, and bracelets
8. Reading material
9. Cigarettes
10. Alcohol
11. Relaxation tapes, coping statements, therapist's phone number
12. Pets
13. Portable phones

Obviously, some of these items might also be used as methods of distraction. The difference between distractors and safety signals is the way in which they are used. A safety signal is the object carried because just having it on hand makes the person feel safer. A distractor is the object that is used to keep the person's mind off feelings of fear and anxiety.

Alcohol and Other Drugs

It is possible that you use a far more dangerous drug to cope with your panic attacks—alcohol. We now know that many men (more men than women) drink to get through situations in which they might have a panic attack. In fact, from one third to one half of people with alcohol problems started down the long road to alcohol addiction by "self-medicating" anxiety or panic. Using alcohol to cope with panic and anxiety is extremely dangerous. This is because, although alcohol works for a little while, it is likely that the user will become dependent |on the alcohol and require more and more of it. As the person drinks more and more, the anxiety-reducing properties of the alcohol become less and less effective. In fact, the anxiety and depression increase, putting the person in an ever-deepening, downward spiral of addiction. If you drink to control your anxiety, make every effort to stop as soon as possible. Ask your doctor or mental health professional for help.

Other Disorders

Panic attacks occur as a symptom of all types of anxiety disorders, including social phobias, obsessive-compulsive phobias, generalized anxiety, and specific phobias. They are also often present in mood disorders, such as depression. If you experience panic within the context of feelings of sadness, hopelessness, loss of interest, or loss of energy, then consult with your mental health professional to learn if a different treatment is more appropriate.

What Causes Panic and Anxiety?

The question of what causes panic and anxiety is very difficult, and we do not know all the answers yet. Although we will not discuss the causes at length here, because they are discussed in later chapters, we must mention several important points about the causes of panic and anxiety.

First, the research does not suggest that panic attacks are due to a disease or a biological dysfunction. Of course, there are the relatively rare examples previously mentioned, in which a physical condition does result in symptoms that resemble those of a panic attack, such as hyperthyroidism or a tumor on the adrenal gland. However, common panic attacks do not seem to be due to any biological dysfunction.

Many people ask whether panic attacks are due to a chemical imbalance. Chemicals, or neurochemicals, are substances in the central nervous system, including the brain, that are involved in sending nerve impulses. Neurochemicals that have been implicated in panic and anxiety include noradrenalin and serotonin. Although these types of substances may be present in greater amounts during specific anxiety episodes, no evidence suggests that an imbalance in these substances is the original or main cause of panic and anxiety. Some recent evidence based on procedures called Positron Emission Tomography (PET) scans indicates that certain parts of the brain seem to be particularly active in patients with anxiety. However, it is not at all clear whether these findings reflect a function of anxiety or a cause of anxiety. All that can be said for certain at this point is that anxiety and panic involve some physiological changes.

Similarly, our research shows that "cognitive" processes—or what you are thinking—in and of themselves do not cause panic. Once again, cognitive processes or thoughts are heavily involved in panic but are not the sole cause. We describe the involvement of your thoughts in panic attacks in later chapters, as well as the interaction between your thoughts and the physiological processes.

What we do know is that a panic attack seems to be a surge of emotion or fear that by itself, is a normal bodily response. What makes it abnormal is that it occurs at the wrong time, that is, when no real reason to be emotional or afraid is present. Again, the response itself is normal and natural and would be the same kind of reaction you would have if real danger (such as being attacked) was present. It is also normal and natural to become anxious about having another panic attack and to be on guard for it to happen. Anxiety such as this will occur anytime a person feels that something could be dangerous or out of his or her control.

Finally, panic attacks, particularly the first panic attack, seem more likely to occur during stressful times. Research has shown that the most common forms of stress associated with initial panic attacks are interpersonal (such as conflicts with important people in your life) and physical. People commonly report that their first panic attack occurred soon after an allergic reaction to a prescription drug, a bad hangover from drinking too much, or even a "bad trip" from use of illegal drugs. In other words, if someone close to you has died, if you are under pressure at work or at home, if you are having problems with your family, then you are more likely to have a panic attack, if panic is a reaction to which you are susceptible. Some people do not have panic attacks when they are emotional or under stress. Instead, they have other types of reactions to stress, such as headaches, high blood pressure, or ulcers. However, if you are susceptible to panic, then even happy occasions might result in panic attacks if they involve major changes in your life. Stress can be both positive and negative. For example, moving to a new home (even if the home is bigger and nicer), having a baby, or getting married, all can set the occasion for panic attacks in susceptible individuals. This pattern probably explains why panic attacks are more likely to begin in the twenties—when people tend to take on new responsibilities, such as leaving home and starting new careers and relationships. We discuss the causes of panic, anxiety, and stress and how to control these reactions in the chapters to follow.[1]

Do You Fit This Program?

The following list can help you to determine whether or not this treatment is right for you.

Have you had:

- repeated episodes of extreme fear (panic) or a lot of anxious anticipation of experiencing another panic attack?

- at least some panic episodes accompanied by physical sensations and thoughts such as difficulty breathing; choking or smothering sensations; heart palpitations or racing heart; chest pain or discomfort; trembling or shaking; sweating, dizziness, unsteadiness, or faintness;

- hot or cold flashes; nausea or abdominal distress; feelings of unreality, detachment; numbness or tingling; or fears of dying, going crazy, or losing control?

- at least one panic episode that was unexpected or came out of the blue?

- a general state of anxiety, vigilance, or being on edge for the next panic or scary bodily sensation?

---

[1] For a complete account of recent research on the nature and causes of anxiety and panic, you may wish to read Anxiety and Its Disorders: The Nature and Treatment of Anxiety and Panic by David H. Barlow, published in 1988, by Guilford Press, 72 Spring Street, New York, New York 10012.

- a range from none to severe levels of avoidance of different activities and situations in which panic is expected or feared to occur?
- a major problem that revolves around the experience of panic instead of fear of other specific objects; fear of social evaluation, contamination, or self-doubt; or chronic worrying about future events?
- panics not directly attributable to physical (organic) causes?

Alternative Treatments

Consulting other mental health professionals in the past for panic and anxiety does not mean this program is not appropriate for you. We have used this program time and time again with people who have been through many different forms of treatment. However, some consideration must be given to other kinds of treatment that you may be undergoing along with your participation in this program. We recommend that if you begin this program, it should not be combined with other psychotherapy focused specifically on panic. The reason for this is that messages from different treatments for the same problem can become mixed and confusing. Therefore, we find that one treatment at a time is much more effective. On the other hand, if the other program is very general or focuses on a different problem area, then there is no reason that the other treatment cannot be done along with this program.

If you are involved in another program targeting your panic attacks, we recommend that you pursue that program until you are sure that either it is effective (in which case no further treatment is needed) or it is ineffective (in which case this program can be tried). As you will soon see, this program has been very effective for many people. That does not mean, however, that other programs will be less effective for you and should not be given a fair trial. Different forms of therapy are more or less effective for different people. You must make this decision if you are involved in another panic treatment program.

Are You Taking Drugs for Your Anxiety?

If you use drugs for the control of anxiety and panic, this program will still be appropriate, if you still have panic attacks or some anxiety about having more panic attacks. For some people, drugs are only mildly to moderately effective or not effective at all. For others, drugs are effective initially, but then relapse occurs when the drug is stopped.

Drug treatments can be successfully combined with this program. In addition, this program has been helpful for persons who want to stop their medications. If you have an interest in stopping the drugs you are taking, this Workbook provides some points to consider later in the Workbook. These can be combined with direct medical supervision of the withdrawal process. It is definitely not wise to stop taking medication on your own.

What Benefits Will You Receive From This Program?

What should you expect to get out of this program? This information is important in your decision to participate in this program. Research studies have been conducted at our Center for Stress and Anxiety Disorders to evaluate our panic-treatment program. The results suggest that this treatment is very successful. The percentage of people who report that they are free of panic at the completion of a program similar to this one is 80%–90%. This rate of success has been replicated in other centers that have tested treatments similar to this one. Even more exciting is that these results seem to persist over long periods of time—up to 24 months after treatment, which is the longest period we have examined. One of the reasons for this maintenance effect is that the treatment is essentially a learning program. When you learn something, it becomes a natural part of your reactions, and, therefore, you carry the learning with you even after you have completed the formal program.

On the basis of the results to date, the National Institute of Mental Health came issued an official statement in September, 1991, recognizing that the treatments of choice for panic disorder are the type of cognitive–behavior therapy provided in this Workbook, or medication therapy, or both. Obviously, there is never a guarantee that this treatment will be the one for you or that you may never panic again, but the success rates indicate that this program is worth trying if you have panic attacks.

As previously mentioned, many people who panic develop agoraphobic avoidance as well. Treatment programs, similar to the one in this Workbook, focused on agoraphobic avoidance per se produce significant improvements in 60%–80% of patients treated. Again, this rate of improvement was maintained, and, in fact, improvement often continued, up to 2 years after treatment completion. In combination with the treatment of panic described in this Workbook, it is likely that this success rate for agoraphobia treatment will increase even more. We also know that including someone from your own family or circle of friends can help you with some of the exercises. The treatment of agoraphobia is described in more detail in the agoraphobia supplement to this program. More about that later.

What Costs Will You Pay?

You now know how effective these programs have been. The question for you, then, is what is the cost? The main costs are time and effort. The next 10–12 weeks will require motivation. One factor (perhaps the only one) known to predict the effectiveness of this program is the amount of practice that you do.

The more you practice, the more you will get out of the program. It is not the severity of your panic and avoidance, how long you have been panicking, or how old you are that predicts success. Instead, it is your motivation to change your reactions. Therefore, this is another decision for you to make—Do you have the motivation at this time to give it your best? One point to keep in mind is that you are probably expending as much energy and effort trying to manage your life with the panic and anxiety as you would going through this program. The big advantage of this program is that the energy and effort result in positive changes.

Even if you have decided that the benefits seem to outweigh the costs in general, you might still have some doubts about the program—You might be concerned about whether or not this program will help you. This is a particularly likely concern if you have tried other programs without success. However, that judgment should be based on how you progress as you go through the program. Even if you have strong doubts now, do not make judgments at this point—Wait until you have given the program a fair trial.

If you do not have the motivation right now, then you will do better to wait. You will be defeating yourself by beginning a program like this halfheartedly.

Finally, if your fear and anxiety diminish quickly as you proceed through the program, we recommend that you still finish the program. The treatment will prove more effective in the long run if you complete the entire series of exercises, in the same way that it is more effective to complete a prescription of an antibiotic even though symptoms have cleared up.

Figure 1.1 on the next page presents the decision points in deciding whether or not the MAP–II program is for you.

Brief Description of the Program

The title of this Workbook is *Mastery of Your Anxiety and Panic—Second Edition* (MAP–II). In this program, you will learn to control your out-of-control fearful emotions. The program consists of 15 chapters or lessons. In each chapter, you will learn specific skills. The skills build on each other, so that in each new lesson, you will use skills you have learned previously. The program is obviously structured, but there is room for individual tailoring because individual differences are very important.

At the end of each chapter is a self-assessment section to determine if you have learned the information. If you have not, go back over the material again. This point is important because each new step is based on the previous steps. If you have understood the material presented in the chapter, then continue to the next.

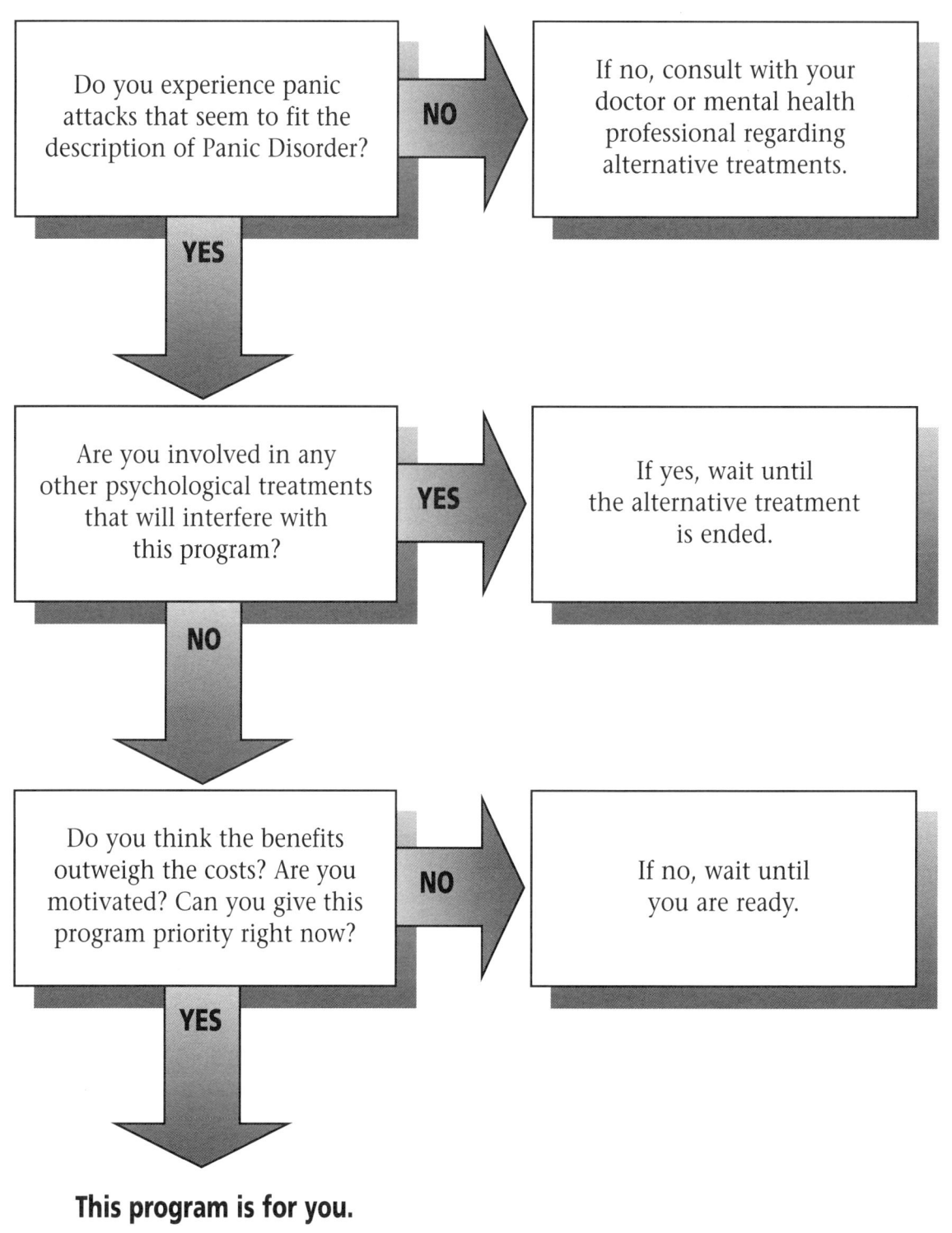

Figure 1.1. Decision Tree

In addition, at the end of each chapter are specific exercises. We cannot overemphasize their importance because the success of the program is based largely on your doing those exercises.

The pace is somewhat up to you, but we recommend intervals of time at the end of each chapter before proceeding to the next. The main issue is for you to conduct the exercises thoroughly before beginning the next chapter.

Finally, we recommend that you work on this program with your doctor or mental health professional. That person can provide additional information, advice, and guidance as you learn the various skills and conduct the different exercises. Furthermore, your doctor or mental health professional can help to tailor the program to your own needs.

This program focuses on teaching control of your panic and anxiety. If you are restricted by agoraphobic avoidance behaviors, we recommend that you complete the MAP–II program first and then proceed to the agoraphobia supplement. The MAP–II program leads you through the following steps:

- Deciding if the program is appropriate for you at this time
- Learning about your reactions
- Developing a perspective for changing your reactions
- Learning what produces panic feelings and gaining corrective information about panic
- Learning physical control
- Developing control of physical responses
- Learning self-statement analysis
- Developing control of self-statements
- Predicting the unexpected
- Producing the panic sensations and learning emotional control
- Producing panic sensations in your daily life and continuing development of emotional control
- Developing further emotional control
- Overcoming phobic avoidance
- Learning about medication issues
- Evaluating yourself and planning maintenance

For the period of time that you give to this program, it must become a priority. Up until this time, fear has been your major focus. Now, achieving mastery of your anxiety and panic should be the major focus.

Self-Assessment

Answer by circling **T** (True) or **F** (False). Answers are provided in Appendix A.

1. It is possible for people to have panic attacks but not meet criteria for the diagnosis of Panic Disorder. **T F**

2. In addition to the unpleasant physical sensations that occur during a panic attack, people experiencing panic attacks often have thoughts that they are going crazy, losing control, or dying. **T F**

3. Panic attacks and panic attacks accompanied by agoraphobic avoidance are not very common problems. **T F**

4. Distracting oneself from fearful sensations and situations is a good method for coping with panic attacks. **T F**

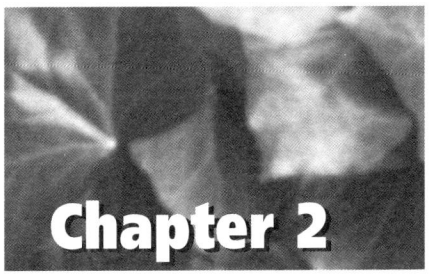

Chapter 2

Learning About Your Reactions

Why Should You Learn to Be an Observer?

A large part of the feeling of loss of control stems from being carried along by emotions without ever stepping outside of the emotional cycle and observing it. To begin change, you must first become aware of what typically occurs and what needs to be changed. Change requires that you become a behavioral scientist rather than a victim in the jungle of your emotions, awaiting the next attack. Observation of your reactions means carefully monitoring when an emotion occurs, under what circumstances it occurs, and the sequence of events. Then, you will be in a position to make more valid judgments about what is going on, to use appropriate methods of change, and to evaluate the effectiveness of your methods.

Tailoring the program to your needs is based very much on how well a given strategy works for you. This information comes from observational records. Studies have consistently shown that general descriptions of emotional reactions recorded some time after they have occurred are much less accurate than on-the-spot accounts of what is felt and what has happened. This difference occurs because our memories are colored by our mood. If you are generally anxious you will remember events as being scarier than they were at the time. Similarly, feeling depressed results in recalling more negative, sad events than positive ones. The biasing effect of mood on memory is part of the reason that fear continues. We will talk more about this effect later. Direct, on-the-spot observation plays a therapeutic role in breaking that cycle. If you monitor emotional events as they occur, you are more likely to think about and remember them accurately, which will help to remove some of the biasing effects of memory.

With on-the-spot monitoring, you can accomplish several extremely important things:

- Identifying conditions in which panic attacks are likely to occur: This information highlights important factors for treatment. Does the panic occur when you are alone or with others, after a stressful day at work or on weekends, in the middle of the day or at the end of the day?

- Identifying specific triggers for the panic: This step is a major task and may be very difficult at first. However, it is a crucial step that lets you begin to break the perception of being the victim of an unpredictable or uncontrollable event that descends upon you when you least expect it. You may discover specific triggers such as feeling excited by a sports event on television, feeling overheated by a crowded shopping area, feeling suffocation from a steamy shower, thinking about horrible things that could happen as a result of becoming anxious, or relaxing and having nothing else to do but dwell on your fears.

- Monitoring that allows you to evaluate your progress: The monitoring continues throughout the entire program. When you are anxious, it is easy to dismiss gains and focus instead on still feeling afraid or having difficulties. On-the-spot monitoring helps you counter that bias in thinking and appreciate the gains you make. Also, when one panic attack makes you feel as though you have failed or fallen back, the monitoring forms provide a context in which to place that panic attack and therefore not allow it to overshadow the progress you have made.

- Gaining control: Monitoring is the first step.

What To Monitor

Panic Attacks

You should monitor panic attacks using the portable Panic Attack Record that is included in the MAP–II Monitoring Forms packet. This form should be used every time you have what you consider to be a panic attack or a sudden rush of fear. Remember, panic is distinguished from anxiety. Panic represents an abrupt surge of fear that may occur out of a deeply relaxed state or a very anxious state. Panic usually peaks quickly and then subsides within 10–30 minutes, although you may continue to feel some of the symptoms and to feel generally anxious for quite a while afterward. Sometimes a panic attack can set off a cycle of intense anxiety and more panic attacks. Nevertheless, the main feature of a panic attack is that it is a sudden or abrupt surge of fear that subsides relatively quickly. In contrast, anxiety tends to build more slowly and to be more generalized. We discuss this more later.

Do not wait until the end of the day to complete the monitoring form. If you wait, you will lose accuracy and lose the sense of being an observer. Complete it as soon as possible after you recognize the panic attack. Some circumstances, such as driving or talking in a meeting, make it hard to stop and fill out the form, but the monitoring should be done as soon as possible afterward.

On the monitoring form, note the date, the time of onset, and duration of the panic. Note with whom it occurred and whether the situation you were in was stressful or not. Give a brief description of the stressful event. Identify whether the panic was expected or unexpected and the maximum level of fear that you experienced. Rate your level of fear on a scale from 0 to 8, where 0 = *no fear*, 2 = *mild fear*, 4 = *moderate fear*, 6 = *strong fear*, and 8 = *extreme fear*. Then, from the list of symptoms, underline the first one you noticed and check off each symptom that was at least mildly present.

Panic Attack Record

Date 2 / 16 / 97 Time Began 5:20 A.M./(P.M.) Duration: 15 (mins.)

With: ☒ Alone ☐ Friend ☐ Stranger ☐ Family

Stressful Situation? ☒ Yes ☐ No *Waiting for husband to come home from work*

Expected? ☒ Yes ☐ No

Maximum Fear *(circle)*

0	1	2	3	4	5	(6)	7	8
None		Mild		Moderate		Strong		Extreme

Symptoms *(underline the first symptom and check all symptoms present):*

- ☒ Difficulty Breathing
- ☒ <u>Racing/Pounding Heart</u>
- ☐ Choking Sensations
- ☒ Sweating
- ☒ Trembling/Shaking
- ☐ Nausea/Abdominal Upset
- ☒ Fear of Losing Control/Going Crazy
- ☐ Chest Pain/Discomfort
- ☐ Hot/Cold Flashes
- ☒ Numbness/Tingling
- ☒ Feelings of Unreality
- ☐ Unsteadiness/Dizziness/Fainting
- ☐ Fear of Dying

Copyright © 1994 by Graywind Publications, Inc. Mastery of Your Anxiety and Panic 0158131541

Figure 2.1. Jill's First Panic Attack Record

Let's examine the records completed by Jill. Jill is 29 years old, married, and the mother of one child. She began to panic one year ago, when her child was a few months old. Since then she has been afraid to stay home alone with her baby and often spends the day at her mother's place while her husband is at work.

According to Jill's first record (see Figure 2.1), this panic occurred at 5:20 p.m. on February 16 and lasted for 15 minutes. She panicked while she was waiting for her husband to return from work, and Jill related the panic to the stressful situation of being alone. It was an expected panic; that is, Jill was not surprised that it happened at this time. Her maximum fear level was 6, which is strong. A racing heart was the first symptom she noticed and, during the panic, other symptoms included difficulty breathing, sweating, trembling and shaking, numbness or

Panic Attack Record

Date 2 / 19 / 97 Time Began 3:00 (A.M.)/P.M. Duration: 5 (mins.)

With: ☐ Alone ☐ Friend ☐ Stranger ☒ Family

Stressful Situation? ☐ Yes ☒ No *Sleeping*

Expected? ☐ Yes ☒ No

Maximum Fear *(circle)*

0	1	2	3	4	5	6	(7)	8
None		Mild		Moderate		Strong		Extreme

Symptoms *(underline the first symptom and check all symptoms present):*

- ☒ Difficulty Breathing
- ☒ <u>Racing/Pounding Heart</u>
- ☐ Choking Sensations
- ☒ Sweating
- ☒ Trembling/Shaking
- ☐ Nausea/Abdominal Upset
- ☐ Fear of Losing Control/Going Crazy
- ☐ Chest Pain/Discomfort
- ☐ Hot/Cold Flashes
- ☐ Numbness/Tingling
- ☐ Feelings of Unreality
- ☐ Unsteadiness/Dizziness/Fainting
- ☒ Fear of Dying

Copyright © 1994 by Graywind Publications, Inc. Mastery of Your Anxiety and Panic 0158131541

Figure 2.2. Jill's Second Panic Attack Record

tingling, feelings of unreality and a fear of losing control or going crazy. According to her second record (see Figure 2.2), this panic occurred at 3:00 A.M. on February 19 and lasted for 5 minutes. Jill panicked out of sleep. She woke up feeling very hot and sweaty and noticed her heart racing. In fact, the raciness of her heart seemed to wake her out of sleep. It was not a stressful situation, and the attack was unexpected. Her maximum fear level was 7. She first noticed the racing heart and then experienced difficulty breathing, sweating, shaking, and fear of dying.

Anxiety

In addition to panic attacks, it is important to monitor general levels of anxiety and other moods. As described in the previous chapter, anxiety about the recurrence of panic is probably the most important feature of panic disorder.
The Daily Mood Record lets you record your levels of anxiety and depression at the end of each day. We find it most helpful to use a scale from 0 to 8 points for rating levels of anxiety, levels of depression, and worry about having a panic attack during the day. For all ratings, 8 is the extreme end of the scale: extreme anxiety, extreme depression ,and extreme anticipation of panic. These ratings are based on how you felt on average during the day. One of these records will last for over a week; a 15-week supply is included in your MAP–II Monitoring Forms packet.

By now, you should realize that panic attacks are different from just being nervous or anxious. It is worth repeating this, though, so you will not confuse the two when using the Panic Attack Record and Daily Mood Record forms. Panic attacks are the sudden surges of frightening emotion experienced by Steve and Susan as illustrated in the first chapter. Even if a person is generally anxious or apprehensive during the day, it is possible for that person to have a sudden surge of panic on top of the anxiety. In fact, these two often go together in this way. Alternatively, a panic attack may come "out of the blue," even when you are asleep and presumably relaxed.

On the other hand, nearly everyone knows what it means to be anxious. Being anxious or nervous or "worrying" quite a bit is something most of us have done. At times this anxiety may be very intense and severe, as it would be when making a speech in front of strangers. In fact, many people would probably be very anxious all day long before this speech, but this anxiety would be different from the sudden surge of emotion that is a panic attack. Anxiety is best described as worrying about something that will happen in the future, even if the future is only an hour away. Panic, on the other hand, is a surge of emotion usually associated with thoughts of dying or losing control at the present time. In this way, a person can be anxious about having a panic attack. We will talk more about the nature and causes of anxiety and panic in Chapters 3 and 4.

According to Jill's Daily Mood Record (see Figure 2.3), over the course of the week, she had a changing pattern of anxiety, depression, and worry about having a panic attack. On February 16 and 17, Jill was quite worried about having a panic

Daily Mood Record

See Figure 2.3 in your workbook.

```
0     1     2     3     4     5     6     7     8
None        Mild        Moderate    Strong      Extreme
```

For each day, rate your anxiety, depression, and anticipation/worry according to the scale above.

Date	Average anxiety	Average depression	Average anticipation/worry about panic
2/16	5	4	6
2/17	6	4	6
2/18	4	3	5
2/19	3	2	4
2/20	4	4	4
2/21	3	2	2
2/22	2	2	2

Copyright © 1994 Graywind Publications, Inc.   Mastery of Your Anxiety and Panic

Figure 2.3. **Jill's Daily Mood Record**

attack; these were the first two days after a weekend spent with her husband. Notice how she was also generally more anxious and depressed on those days compared to other days. In contrast, on February 21 and 22 (the weekend), she felt less anxious, less depressed, and less worried about panicking because her husband was with her the whole time.

Over the course of several weeks, important trends usually become evident. One example is the way moods fluctuate in relation to the frequency of panic attacks. It will be important to learn this information to make your treatment as effective as possible.

Progress

It is helpful to keep a chart of your improvement based on these monitoring forms. The Progress Record is divided into the number of panics per week and the average anxiety per week (calculate your average anxiety by adding all of your anxiety ratings for the past week and dividing that sum by the number of times you rated your anxiety for the past week). Of course, you may also record other dimensions (such as worry about panic or level of depressed mood) in which you are interested. This Progress Record, like the one shown in Figure 2.4, will allow you to see how you are doing and to put things into perspective. It is helpful to keep this in a visible place, such as on your bathroom mirror or on the refrigerator door. Use the Progress Record form included in your MAP–II Monitoring Forms packet.

Activities and Places

We have not discussed the monitoring of your activities and your ability to go places on your own. We discuss agoraphobic avoidance in more detail in the *Agoraphobia Supplement to the MAP–II Program*. This supplement is best tackled after finishing the MAP–II program, which focuses on controlling your panic and avoidance.

Summary

The importance of this monitoring cannot be overemphasized. You must do it daily to get the full benefit from this program. Although, at first, you may have to push yourself to monitor, it will become easier and even rewarding. The monitoring helps to give yourself feedback. It is also beneficial for your mental health professional if you provide this kind of information. These records will be invaluable during the rest of the program, so monitoring is definitely worth the effort.

Sometimes people ask why they should monitor their reactions, considering that they spend almost all the time being overly aware of feeling anxious and their bodily symptoms anyway. The monitoring seems to feed into the cycle of fear

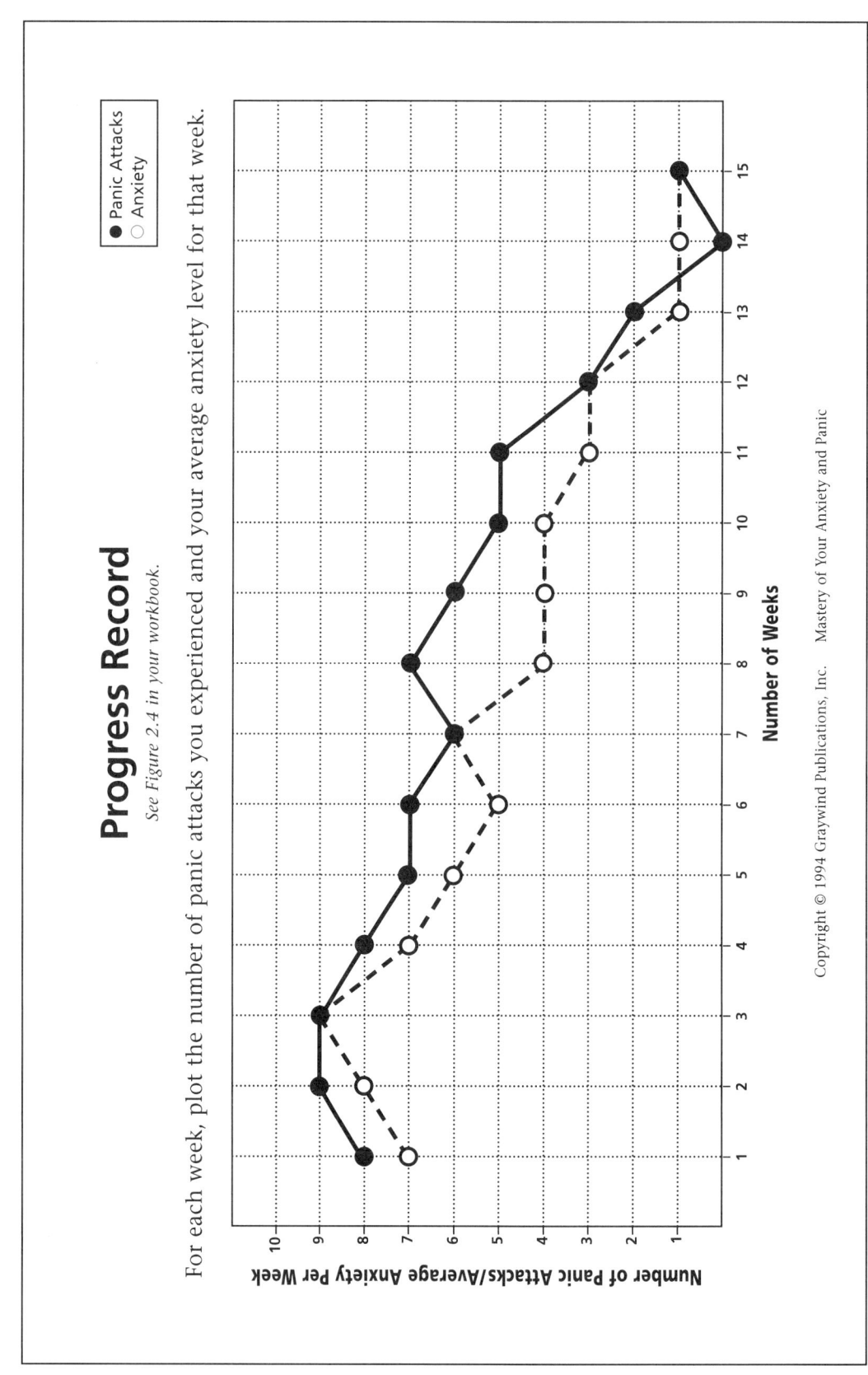

Figure 2.4. **Progress Record**

and anxiety. However, the self-monitoring described in this chapter emphasizes the development of an objective awareness. Being an objective observer is very different from being anxiously preoccupied, which is reflected by statements such as "I don't feel well, I could panic today, what if I get so dizzy that I have to go home. . . ." Instead, the objective approach is reflected by statements such as "My anxiety level is moderate, and my physical symptoms include dizziness. This panic episode occurred in relation to the stress of rushing to get everything done on time." In the next few chapters, we add objective monitoring of your thoughts to the list of things of which you must become fully aware. Only this awareness allows change to take place.

Exercise

Monitor your panics and daily mood levels for a full week using the forms in your packet. Do not start other parts of the program yet because you are still learning about your reactions. This next week of daily monitoring will be a good test of your motivation.

Self-Assessment

Answer by circling **T** (True) or **F** (False). Answers are provided in Appendix A.

1. Monitoring is important because it provides a more accurate description of your fear than do vague generalities or trying to remember events from the past.   **T   F**

2. It is best not to think about how anxious you feel.   **T   F**

3. Monitoring of panics is best done at the end of the day.   **T   F**

4. Monitoring is essential for the identification of conditions and triggers that provoke panic.   **T   F**

5. Monitoring of anxiety and other moods can wait until the end of the day.   **T   F**

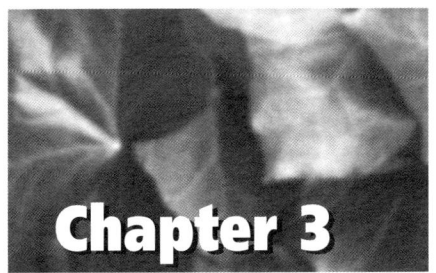

Chapter 3

Developing a Perspective for Changing Your Reactions

Review

Did you complete a mood record every day and record panics as they occurred? If not, try to think of ways of improving your ability to self-monitor, because self-monitoring is essential to the program. Remember, change depends on a complete and accurate awareness of the nature of the problem. It is impossible to change without knowing exactly what it is that has to change. In addition, self-monitoring becomes more important as you proceed through the steps in the next few chapters. Getting into the habit of self-monitoring now will help you complete the rest of the program.

To help you remember to complete the records, place the Daily Mood Record in a visible place, such as on the refrigerator. Also, carry your Panic Attack Records with you wherever you go.

If you have not done any monitoring, we strongly recommend that you use the following week to monitor before continuing with the program.

If you have monitored over the last week, look at the patterns that have emerged. For instance, do the panics typically occur when you are alone or when you are with someone? Do they occur at a particular time of the day, such as in the evening when you are watching television? Do they occur more often in stressful situations than in nonstressful ones? Are the symptoms the same each time or do they vary depending on where the panic occurs? Is the first symptom the same each time? In addition, look for relationships between what you recorded on the Panic Attack Record and the Daily Mood Record. For instance, does panic occur more often when you are feeling generally more anxious or depressed? Does your anxious anticipation of panic increase after a panic or before a panic? Now that the week of monitoring is over, fill in the data for the first week on the Progress

Record: number of panics for the week, average daily anxiety rating for the week, and whatever other information you decide to chart.

Looking for patterns is the first step in learning that the feeling of panic is a reaction. It is not some automatic response over which you have no control. Calling it a "reaction" means there is something you can do to change or learn in order to react differently. It is this aspect that we begin to examine shortly. First, we discuss the nature of anxiety. In the next chapter, we can focus more on the experience of panic.

What Is Anxiety?

Anxiety is a natural emotion that is experienced by everyone. Anxiety is part of the experience of being human. Anxiety is not bad in and of itself, and it can be a productive, driving force. Research over the years has shown that having some anxiety enhances performance. That is, you do better at what you are doing, whether in the classroom or on the tennis court, when anxiety is present up to a certain level. However, anxiety can vary in severity, from mild uneasiness to extreme distress. It can also vary in frequency, from occasional distress to seemingly constant unease. When anxiety is very intense or very frequent, it can interfere with daily life. Hence, the goal of this program is for you to reduce the frequency or intensity of anxiety, or both, at times when it is inappropriate. However, the goal is not to remove anxiety altogether, because that is impossible and also undesirable. Some anxiety is good and is needed in certain situations or for certain levels of performance.

Viewing anxiety along a scale from none to extreme, place yourself on that scale in terms of how you feel generally (as you have been doing by keeping a Daily Mood Record). You are likely to place yourself toward the extreme end of the scale. That is, your anxiety is likely to be at a level that is higher than you want. For that reason, the anxiety feels as though it is out of your control. This program will help you bring that level down to a point where you feel comfortable and, yet, still have some anxiety under certain conditions without feeling as if it is out of your control.

Anxiety is difficult to manage when viewed as a whole or as a "lump." A "lump" approach does not provide clues for controlling anxiety. It is easy for other people to say "stop being so anxious, just relax," but it is difficult to use that advice as a method of control. When anxiety is viewed in terms of its components, however, learning to become less anxious is much easier. In addition, the concept of anxiety as a reaction becomes more understandable.

What are the major components of anxiety and panic? The three major components are physiology, thoughts, and behaviors. Here is an explanation of each one.

The physiology component involves the physical sensations or symptoms, such as muscle tension, a rapid pulse, difficulty breathing, a nervous stomach possibly accompanied by diarrhea, frequent or excessive sweating, tremulousness, headaches, stomachaches, a lump in the throat, frequent urination, visual disturbances, a sense of pressure in the head, and many, many more. The physical symptoms can be acute, lasting a short period of time (as in panic attacks) or can be prolonged, lasting hours or days (as in chronic anxiety).

The thoughts or statements of anxiety involve a sense of impending doom, thoughts that something terrible is about to happen, a sense of danger, and worrying about the present and future. It is the anticipation of the worst and the apprehension about what is going to happen. It is the feeling that events could proceed uncontrollably or that you may not have control over your reactions. It is a feeling of helplessness in the face of uncertainty.

The behavior component refers to what you do. It involves pacing up and down, restlessness, and fidgeting. It also involves escaping from or avoiding places or events where anxiety or panic is expected to occur. An example of escaping is to leave a shopping mall as soon as the feelings of anxiety or panic develop. An example of avoiding is to shy away from talking to people because of anxiety about how they may react or how they may evaluate what you say. At a more subtle level, the behavior may entail looking for exits to decrease the sense of being trapped, or relying on objects or situations that make you feel safer (these are the safety signals that we described in the previous chapter). For example, a behavior might be to remain close to another person or to some type of railing for fear of falling down. Poor concentration is sometimes a behavior of anxiety and panic. However, it is important to note that anxiety and panic do not lessen the capacity to concentrate; instead, they shift the focus of attention and concentration. So, if you are worrying about passing an exam, your concentration on the possibility of failure may interfere with your concentration on the exam questions. This interference thereby creates the sense of a lack of concentration.

The components of physiology, thoughts and behaviors may vary in their relative importance from one person to another. They may even vary in importance within a person at different times. For some, physiology may be more important than the behavior. For example, one person may experience a lot of physical tension, headaches, and diarrhea but continue to do most things. Another may stay at home as much as possible in order to avoid any uncomfortable physical symptoms but, as a result, experience little actual physical discomfort. In addition, sometimes the physiology component may be the most dominant, whereas thoughts may become more important on another occasion. For example, stomach discomfort may be the strongest factor on one occasion, while worrying about feeling embarrassed may be stronger on another occasion. Similarly, dizziness may be the strongest component when driving on a freeway, when worries about going crazy may be stronger when home alone. Despite the variations in the importance of each component, each plays a role in the experience of anxiety.

In the previous chapter, we described anxiety as being generally nervous about something bad that might happen. In contrast, a panic attack is a sudden surge of fear. Try to distinguish the feeling of anxiety from the feeling of panic. Think about how you feel when you are generally anxious (such as when you are worrying about having a panic attack in the future or worrying about finishing a project). Now, describe the physical, thought, and behavioral components of your anxiety on the Anxiety Components Form in your MAP–II Monitoring Forms packet. That is, record what you typically feel, what you think, and what you do when you are anxious on the Anxiety Components Form.

Remember Jill? Figure 3.1 shows how she completed her Anxiety Components Form. The physiology, thoughts, and behaviors that characterize her general anxiety are provided as an example. Much of Jill's general anxiety involves worrying about having enough time during the day to get everything done. She also worries about the health of her child and of her husband (her thoughts). When anxious, she experiences a lot of muscle tension and headaches (her physical sensations). Also, she often bites her nails and puts things off (her behavior).

Now, on the Panic Components Form in your MAP–II Monitoring Forms packet, record the same information for your panic attacks. Record what you feel, what you typically think, and what you do when you panic. Jill's example is shown in Figure 3.2.

Anxiety Components

See Figure 3.1 in your workbook.

Major physical sensations:
1. Muscle tension and stiffness
2. Headaches

Major thoughts:
1. I won't get everything done on time.
2. Maybe my son or husband will get sick.

Major behaviors:
1. Nail biting
2. Procrastination

Copyright © 1994 Graywind Publications, Inc.   Mastery of Your Anxiety and Panic

---

Figure 3.1. **A Completed Anxiety Components Form**

What you are recording for panic attacks probably differs from what you recorded on the Anxiety Components Form. For example, the anxiety thoughts may center on worrying about future events, in contrast to panic thoughts that center on worrying about immediate danger, such as heart attack or suffocation. Similarly, the behaviors are probably different: In anxious states, the behavior may involve fidgeting and pacing, whereas in panic, the behaviors may entail immediate escape and avoidance. The physiologic component in general anxiety may involve muscle tension, in contrast to numbness and weakness during panic. Use your Panic Attack Records to help you identify your major physical symptoms, thoughts, and behaviors when you panic. Jill's list of panic responses is provided as an example (Figure 3.2). As you can see, her sensations, thoughts, and behaviors when panicking are very different from her sensations, thoughts, and behaviors when she feels anxious.

So, both anxiety and panic have three major components: First is the physiological arousal that is associated with physical sensations or feelings. Second are the thoughts, or things that you say to yourself (self-statements); beliefs; interpretations; expectations; and imagery. Third are the behaviors that include avoidance and escape from frightening situations and perhaps disruption of concentration.

It is important to recognize that the different components (physiology, thoughts, and behaviors) are partially independent but are also interactive. That is, they can

---

Panic Components

See Figure 3.2 in your workbook.

Major physical sensations:
1. Racing heart
2. Dizziness

Major thoughts:
1. I'm losing control.
2. This may never end.

Major behaviors:
1. Escape-go to home or to mother's place
2. Don't go to certain places

Copyright © 1994 Graywind Publications, Inc.   Mastery of Your Anxiety and Panic

Figure 3.2.   A Completed Panic Components Form

occur separately at times, although they usually interact. For example, you may feel a racing heart and shaky feelings, and, yet, continue to drive to the next town. In this case, there is a discrepancy between the physical and behavioral components; despite the physical symptoms, the behavior is of continued approach instead of avoidance. However, the three components interact with each other as well. For example, negative thoughts may directly increase one's level of physical tension. If you tell yourself that a dangerous event is about to occur, then it makes sense that your level of physical tension will increase. Similarly, attempting to escape a crowd of people can increase the level of physical arousal as well. Furthermore, physical arousal is likely to increase the likelihood that anxious negative thoughts will come to mind.

In fact, the interactions among these three components create a cycling effect, resulting in increased anxiety. For example, negative thoughts may bring about increased physiological arousal. This may, in turn, interfere with concentration on a task. In other words, worrying about getting all of your work completed may result in agitation and restlessness. These can then interfere with your concentration on the work, with the lack of concentration thus delaying completion of the project. As a result, there is likely to be further worry about the consequences of not getting the job done on time, and the anxious cycle continues. Another example typical of panic attacks is misinterpretations about physical sensations—Thinking that a racing heart is a sign of heart disease results in increased fearfulness. This, in turn, intensifies the physical sensations, as fear increases arousal. This panic cycle is discussed much further in the next chapter.

Therefore, these three components often interact in ways that create further anxiety and fear or panic. Being aware of the way in which the components feed off each other to create anxiety and panic can be useful. Think about a recent anxiety episode and the sequence of events that led to the high point of the anxiety. Remember, anxiety is separate from panic. What was the first thing that happened? Was it physical tension? Was it a thought that something bad could happen in the future? Was it procrastination? Describe the sequence of responses to yourself. For example, Jill experienced a high level of anxiety on a Friday afternoon when she was at her mother's house. Her child was at a friend's place for a party, and her husband was at work. After she took her son to the party, Jill began to feel anxious because she was concerned about something—anything—happening to him while she was not there to protect him. At her mother's place, Jill watched a newscast about some children who had been kidnapped. Her immediate reaction was to think more about the safety of her own child. This thinking spiraled into worrying about the safety of her husband. She began to pace and feel agitated and worry more about the safety of her family, with images of being left on her own and not being able to cope. This, in turn, produced further agitation, restlessness, sweating, and a headache. She tried to concentrate on reading but kept going back to the worries in her mind. Here, the sequence of events was a self-statement that something bad could happen, followed by physiological arousal, followed by further worry, followed by further arousal, and so on.

Perform the same kind of sequential analysis for one of your own recent anxiety episodes. Look at the episode as an observer rather than simply stating that you felt anxious. Remember, the analysis is not only questioning of the original cause of the anxiety but also analysis of the sequence through which the anxiety developed. Why does anxiety become more severe or more enduring at any given time? Why did Jill's anxiety not subside immediately? It was because she added to her worries about her son and husband with further agitation, arousal and further concern. Alternatively, she could have interrupted the anxiety spiral early on with some of the methods we discuss later.

Now, perform the same analysis for recent panic attacks. What was the first thing that happened? What followed? How did the fear spiral? Use the following examples to help you analyze the sequence of your own experiences:

> **Physically, my head felt really light, and my hands were clammy. I thought that either I would pass out or that I would somehow dissolve into nothingness. My behavioral response was to lie down and call my husband who was at work.**

> **The very first thing I felt was when I stood up—my head started to feel really weird, as if it was spinning inside. My next reaction was to hold onto the chair. I thought something was wrong. I thought it could get worse and worse and I would collapse. So, by then I was feeling pretty anxious. As the dizziness got worse and worse I became really concerned, because it was different from any other experience I had ever had. I was convinced that this was "it." That's when I called my husband, and lay down waiting for him to arrive. Now, in retrospect I see how my thoughts about what could happen made everything that much worse.**

Some examples from Jill's analyses of panic sequences are provided in Figure 3.3.

Do the same kind of sequence analyses for three of your recent panic attacks on the Panic Sequences Form in your packet.

Now, you have begun to develop a new perspective.

How Does It All Begin?

As we noted previously, understanding the causes of anxiety or panic attacks is not necessary to benefit from treatment, but it is helpful. It is not necessary because factors that are responsible for the initial onset of a problem are not necessarily the same as those responsible for the maintenance of the problem. For example, an initial panic attack may occur within the context of marital problems, but the panic continues after these marital problems have been

Panic Sequences

See Figure 3.3 in your workbook.

Panic #		Sequence
1.	a.	at home watching TV
	b.	felt heart flutter
	c.	focused on my heart and worried about heart attack
	d.	heart rate sped up
	e.	convinced I was in danger
	f.	called my husband and asked him to come home
2.	a.	in restaurant with family
	b.	thought "I'd be really embarrassed if I panicked here"
	c.	began to feel numb all over
	d.	thought I would panic and have to run out of restaurant
	e.	lost my appetite
	f.	asked husband and son to eat quickly so we could leave
3.	a.	in shopping mall
	b.	felt dizzy and lightheaded
	c.	looked for exit and felt trapped
	d.	walked quickly to end of mall
	e.	heart rate speeding
	f.	thought I would faint

Copyright © 1994 Graywind Publications, Inc.   Mastery of Your Anxiety and Panic

Figure 3.3.   A Completed Panic Sequences Form

resolved. This continuation occurs because panic attacks and anxiety tend to take on a cycle of their own. It is that cycle that the MAP–II program breaks.

Patients often ask whether there are genetic factors in anxiety and panic. That is, are anxiety and panic inherited? This is an area of research that is advancing quickly. It seems that there is an inherited component to being anxious or tense. On the other hand, having an inherited component does not necessarily mean that an individual inherits a problem with anxiety or a specific anxiety disorder. An individual does not inherit agoraphobia or a specific phobia, for example. Rather, what is most likely to be inherited is a general sensitivity. Furthermore, this sensitivity most likely contributes to the later development of all the anxiety disorders, as opposed to being specific to one type, such as panic disorder. Finally, it is important to note that what we are calling generalized sensitivity (or strong emotional reactivity) does not necessarily mean anxiety. Generalized sensitivity includes a tendency to experience all emotions strongly, both positive and negative ones, so that you might feel more empathy and compassion than most, or you may be more excitable in a positive way as well. That is, it is possible to be generally sensitive without being overly anxious. Therefore, being emotional and sensitive to good events and bad events is not necessarily a sign of impending anxiety. Nevertheless, as we stated, a general sensitivity, or being "high strung," may contribute to the likelihood of developing an anxiety problem, particularly when stressful life events occur.

Panic attacks typically first occur in the context of a stressful life event. Stress can arise from negative events (such as loss of a job) and from positive events (such as a job promotion). During these stressful periods, a person tends to be sensitized in a way that makes him or her more reactive in general. This sensitization is believed to occur through physical and psychological means. Physically, stress can increase the overall level of arousal, making surges of fearful arousal more likely. Psychologically, stress can increase the sense of vulnerability, which, in turn, lowers the person's perception of her or his ability to control events. Additionally, having to deal with many negative life stressors can generate a sense that the world is a threatening or dangerous place, a perception making it more likely that a panic attack will occur. So, a situation that may be easily dealt with at another time may become anxiety producing at a time of general stress. Think of a person who has recently lost his or her job and whose marriage is breaking up. It would be much more difficult for that person to deal with an "obnoxious" person than if he or she were not suffering such life instability. A bout of the flu might also seem to be more dangerous than it would under other conditions. So, as a result, stress can lead to the experience of specific negative emotions such as panic attacks.

Not everyone who is under stress develops panic attacks. Some people develop other problems in reaction to stress, such as headaches, hypertension, ulcers, or nervous stomachs (irritable bowel syndrome). In fact, there is some evidence that these types of problems also "run in families." For example if your parents or others in your family develop headaches when they are tense, the chances are greater that you will also have headaches. Similarly, if panic attacks run in your family the chances are greater that you will also experience panic if under stress. (This probability is nowhere near 100% but is closer to 30%.) Although the family patterns suggest that panic is inherited, it may be that people learn to panic by watching their parents or others panic in stressful situations.

Finally, even if anxiety and panic are inherited, they are not inherited in the same way that eye color is inherited. If you inherit the genetic structure for blue eyes, then you will have blue eyes. However, inheriting a generalized sensitivity does not mean that you will necessarily become overly anxious or panic-stricken. The reason is that despite a predisposition to anxiety and panic, you can think and act in ways that prevent anxiety or panic from happening.

In any case, a person who may have a predisposition to be generally sensitive might then be sensitized further by stress. This person can then encounter a situation that, during less stressful times, would cause little anxiety. Because of the increased sensitivity, however, the person panics. This first attack may be followed by other panic attacks in various places or situations due to generalization, which we discuss in the next chapter. It is important to realize that panic attacks are in many ways just like other manifestations of stress (headaches and ulcers) and often develop under stressful conditions.

Training Program Rationale

This program will teach you to alter your responses by learning to change the way you think and the way you react physically and behaviorally. In essence, the program involves learning new methods of control. At present, you are most likely intensifying your anxiety because of the "anxious" nature of your thoughts and the "activation" of your physical nervous system.

This program consists of four basic strategies: techniques designed to modify what you say to yourself, techniques designed to control your physical sensations, techniques designed to help you learn new ways of reacting to your physical sensations, and techniques designed to help you face more comfortably places that you fear and avoid. As you master the procedures, you will be better able to understand and deal with anxiety and panic.

We begin with the strategies directed at your thinking or self-statements. Due to the interactive nature of the components of anxiety and panic, changing your thoughts will affect your physiology and your behavior as well. These cognitive strategies involve a detailed understanding of panic attacks and of the kinds of misinterpretations that can contribute to anxiety and panic. You will learn methods of challenging your interpretations and assumptions. Once you are able to isolate the self-statements that often precipitate anxiety and panic, you will learn to treat them as beliefs or hypotheses rather than as facts. The general strategy is to question and challenge these hypotheses by examining the evidence and how you arrived at the conclusions.

The second aspect of the treatment involves learning techniques to control many of your physical sensations. These techniques involve the control of your breathing and muscle tension. Many people breathe too much when they have a panic attack, even though they often feel that the opposite is true. Overbreathing is often a major reason for the physical sensations. Thus, learning to control your breathing will help to reduce many of the panic symptoms. In addition, muscle relaxation is used to maintain physiological calmness if you feel yourself becoming tense or "uptight."

The third part of this treatment involves relearning how to react to physical sensations such as shortness of breath, dizziness, or palpitations. You will learn to be less fearful of those sensations through a set of structured exercises. These will help you to confront the sensations and learn that they are harmless despite your fears. This understanding will help in dealing with panic that seems to come out of the blue and with the anticipation of future panic.

The fourth part of treatment entails practice in the situations that you have been avoiding because of anticipation of panic attacks (i.e., agoraphobic avoidance). Because not everyone who panics develops agoraphobia, this Workbook focuses on the control of panic and anticipatory anxiety about panic. One chapter briefly addresses the methods of overcoming agoraphobia. The Agoraphobia Supplement deals specifically with overcoming agoraphobic avoidance.

It is important to realize that achieving control of your anxiety and panic is a skill that has to be learned. To be effective, these skills must be practiced regularly. In other words, everything you learn in this Workbook must be practiced over and over again until it becomes part of your natural method of responding. You are asked to practice different things at the end of each chapter.

Exercise

Your assignment for this week is to continue to monitor your anxiety and panic, looking for patterns of response and identifying possible triggers. Use the Panic Attack Record and Daily Mood Record from your MAP–II Monitoring Forms packet. In addition, it is important to write down something else about your panic attacks. For each panic attack that occurs, keep a record of the sequence of events that led up to the panic, just as you did before for recent panic attacks. Use the Panic Sequences Form in your packet. Panic attacks may seem to occur all at once, but if you step back and observe, you will discover a sequential process.

Self-Assessment:

Answer by circling **T** (True) or **F** (False). Answers are provided in Appendix A.

1. Anxiety and panic are reactions made up of three major components: physiology, thoughts, and behaviors. **T F**

2. One should never feel anxious. **T F**

3. Physiology, thoughts, and behaviors interact and spiral the emotional state. **T F**

4. Heredity explains all of panic. **T F**

5. Anxiety is different from panic—anxiety is usually anticipation of future events whereas panic is a sudden rush of fear. **T F**

6. The treatment program presented in this Workbook involves teaching you to alter your panic responses by learning to change the way you think and the way you react physically and behaviorally. **T F**

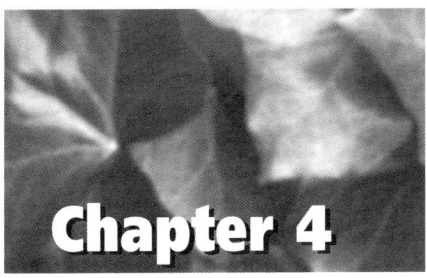

Chapter 4

What Produces the Panic Feelings

Review

Look back over your weekly monitoring from your Daily Mood Record and Panic Attack Record. Examine the patterns of the panic attacks. Has more information emerged from your second week of monitoring? Does the panic occur in specific circumstances? What is the first symptom you typically notice when the panic begins? Analyze the sequence of events from your Panic Sequence Form. What tends to be the first response? The second? What follows? How do the different responses spiral into panic? Remember, the responses are likely to include specific thoughts, behaviors, and physical sensations. Were you able to observe the way in which the three response components fed into each other to create a cycle of panic?

Complete the second week of your Progress Record by charting the average anxiety and number of panics over the last week. Draw a line between each of these two points and the corresponding points from last week. Do not be concerned at this time if the line does not show a reduction. Reduction in panic and anxiety does not typically occur overnight, as changing your reactions is a learning process that occurs with time and practice.

The Physiology of Panic

Although panic, by definition, is unpleasant, it is not in the least dangerous. Panic is a response to danger or threat, whether the danger is perceived or real. Scientifically, panic is termed the fight–flight response or the emergency reaction. It is so named because its effects are aimed toward dealing with an emergency by either fighting or fleeing the danger. Thus, the purpose of panic is to protect the organism. Back in the days when our ancestors lived in caves, it was vital that when they were faced with danger, an automatic response would take over, causing them to take immediate action, to attack or to run. Even in today's hectic world this response is necessary. Imagine you are crossing the street when a car suddenly speeds toward you with its horn blasting. If you experienced no anxiety, you would be killed. However, most likely, your fight–flight response would take over, and you would run to safety. The moral of this story is a simple one—the purpose of panic is to protect the organism, not to harm it.

Thus, the best way to think of the components of panic (the behavior, the physiology and the thoughts) is to remember that they are aimed at preparing you for immediate action, as if you were about to be attacked, and that their purpose is protection. After the fight–flight response occurs in response to actual danger, such as jumping out of the way of a car, you collect yourself, make a mental note, decide to look both ways at that corner in the future, and then go about your business. You would not start worrying about your heart beating too fast or feeling tingly all over. However, if you have a fight–flight surge when there is no real danger, then the response becomes a panic attack. Because you do not know why it is happening, the attack can elicit more anxiety and fear and spiral into a terrifying experience. This is particularly true if something has made you worry about being sick to begin with. For example, did a member of your family recently die of a heart attack? Was your mother always concerned about your health while you were growing up? If so, then health-related concerns may be in the back of your mind, and it is natural that you would think about physical dangers when your body feels out of control during a panic attack. For these reasons, it is important to understand the physiology of panic.

Nervous and Chemical Effects

When some sort of danger is perceived or anticipated, the brain sends messages to a section of your nerves called the autonomic nervous system. The autonomic nervous system has two branches, one called the sympathetic nervous system and one called the parasympathetic nervous system. These two branches of the nervous system are directly involved in controlling the body's energy levels in preparation for action. Simply put, the sympathetic nervous system is the emergency fight–flight response system that releases energy to prepare the body for action. In contrast, the parasympathetic nervous system is the restoring system, which returns the body to a normal state.

One important point is that the sympathetic nervous system tends to be an all-or-nothing system. When it is activated, all of its parts respond quickly. In other words, either all the symptoms of sympathetic activation are experienced or no symptoms are experienced; it is rare for changes to occur in one part of the body alone. This fact may explain why most panic attacks involve many symptoms, and not just one or two.

One of the major effects of the sympathetic nervous system is the release of two chemicals called adrenaline and noradrenaline from the adrenal glands attached to the kidneys. These chemicals are messengers to the body to continue activity, so that once activity in the sympathetic nervous system begins, it often continues and increases for a period of time. However, it is important to note that this activity is stopped in two ways. First, the chemical messengers, adrenaline and noradrenaline, are eventually destroyed by other chemicals in the body. Second, the parasympathetic nervous system, which generally has opposing effects to the sympathetic nervous system, becomes activated and restores the body to a relaxed state. It is important to realize that eventually the body will have enough of the emergency response and will activate the parasympathetic nervous system to restore a state of relaxation. In other words, sympathetic fight–flight arousal cannot continue forever, nor can it spiral to ever-increasing and possibly damaging levels. The parasympathetic nervous system is a built-in protector that stops the sympathetic nervous system from getting carried away. Another important point is that the chemical messengers, adrenaline and noradrenaline, take some time to be completely destroyed. Thus, even after the immediate danger and accompanying surge of emotion have passed and your sympathetic nervous system has stopped responding, you are likely to feel keyed up or apprehensive for some time because the chemicals are still floating around in your system. You must remind yourself that this is natural and harmless. In fact, this is an adaptive function because, in the wild, danger often returns, and it is useful to be prepared to reactivate the emergency response. The panic sensations that become frightening in and of themselves are real sensations—they are not just in your mind. They are real and are almost always physiologically based, but they are not harmful. In fact, they are the result of physical changes that are survival oriented. The question is, Why do the sensations of fight–flight arousal occur when there is no real danger? We discuss this later.

Cardiovascular Effects

Activity in the sympathetic nervous system produces an increase in heart rate and in the strength of the heartbeat. These reactions are vital to preparation for action because they help speed up the blood flow and improve delivery of oxygen to the tissues and the removal of waste from the tissues. These activities are important because oxygen is the energy source for the body. In addition to increased activity in the heart, there is also a change in blood flow. The blood is directed away from places where it is not needed by a tightening of the blood vessels (usually away from the periphery) and toward places where it is needed more, by an expansion of blood vessels (usually toward the big muscle groups in the legs and the heart, etc.). For example, blood is drawn away from the skin, fingers, and toes. Not only does this effect permit more effective use of the important central organs (such as the heart), but it also means that the organism is less likely to bleed as much if attacked. That is because injury is most likely to be sustained in the periphery or the limbs, where the blood flow has been slowed down.

Increased heart rate and redirection of the blood flow are useful in preparation for danger. As a result, certain physical sensations are experienced. In addition to a racing or pounding heart, these changes often include pale and cold skin, cold fingers and toes, and sometimes numbness or feelings of weakness in the hands and feet. You might feel cold even though it is a warm day. These are normal sensations under conditions of anxiety and fear, when the body is preparing for danger, and are not dangerous.

Sometimes people report feeling hot instead of cold when they are distressed. Hot flushes are more likely to occur during the abrupt rush of fear or panic, as the sympathetic nervous system is activated and before the blood flow is redirected. On the other hand, chills that go along with the redirection of the blood flow are more likely to occur with more slowly building or longer lasting anxiety.

Respiratory Effects

The emergency response is associated with an increase in the speed and depth of breathing. This reaction has obvious importance for defense because the tissues need to get more oxygen to prepare for action. The sensations produced by increased breathing can include breathlessness, choking or smothering sensations, dizziness, disorientation, and pain and tightness in the chest. As a side effect of increased breathing, especially if no actual fight–flight activity occurs, the blood supply to the brain is decreased. This is only a small reduction in blood flow to the brain, and it is not at all dangerous. However, it produces some unpleasant symptoms, such as dizziness, blurred vision, and confusion. We discuss the role of respiratory effects in more detail in the next chapter. So, again, adaptive physical changes can produce symptoms that might be uncomfortable but that are not at all harmful.

Sweat Gland Effects

Activation of the emergency response increases sweat gland activity. This effect also has important and useful functions. It cools the body to stop it from overheating, and it makes the skin more slippery, so it is more difficult for a predator to grasp. As a result, perspiration is a very common symptom of anxiety and panic.

Other Physical Effects

A number of other effects are produced by activation of the arousal system. The pupils widen or dilate to let in more light and to extend peripheral vision. This effect facilitates scanning of the environment to search out danger. Remember, anxiety is a response to the perception of threat, and if threat is expected to occur, then it makes sense to be on guard looking for it. The physical side effects of pupil dilation include sensitivity to light, spots in the visual field, and other visual disturbances. Another typical physical change is a decrease in salivation and in digestive processes in general. As a result, it is common to have a dry mouth, to feel nauseous, or to have constipation or a heavy feeling in the stomach. Of course, many muscle groups tense up in preparation for danger, resulting in feelings of tension. This tension can cause pains and aches as well as trembling and shaking. There are many other physical symptoms as well.

Overall, the emergency response results in activation of the whole metabolism and an increased sensitivity to the external environment. Because this process takes a lot of energy, the person generally feels tired, drained, and washed out afterwards.

So, useful physical changes underlie most, if not all, of the physical sensations of panic and anxiety. Therefore, shortness of breath, dizziness, palpitations, and so on are real but not harmful. Occasionally sensations are experienced without actual physical changes taking place. For example, it is not uncommon for people to feel as if their heart is racing when in fact it is beating at a normal pace. This sensation occurs as a result of being fearful of bodily sensations and by monitoring of one's physical state: An intense focus on bodily functions can create the perception of a disturbance when none really exists. However, more intense panic attacks, initial panic attacks, and the majority of panic attacks in general are based on actual physical changes.

The Behavior of Panic

The emergency response prepares the body to either attack or run. Thus, it is no surprise that the overwhelming urge associated with this response is to escape. You may have had the thought, "I've got to get out of here." Sometimes escape is not possible, such as when you are in church in the middle of the pew or at an important meeting. At these times, the urges may become stronger or be shown through such behaviors as foot tapping, pacing, or "snapping" at people.

The Thoughts of Panic

Cognitively, the primary effect of the emergency response is to alert the organism to the possibility of danger. Thus, one of the major effects is an immediate shift in attention to search for potential threat. This effect is an important part of the emergency response: It stops you from attending to your ongoing chores and permits you to scan your surroundings for danger. Sometimes an obvious threat cannot be found. However, most of us cannot accept having no explanation. When an explanation for the anxious feelings cannot be found, the search may be turned inward. In other words, if the person cannot see something outside himself or herself, the he or she assumes that there must be something wrong with him or her. Then, the brain "invents" an explanation such as "I must be dying, losing control, or going crazy." As we have seen, nothing could be further from the truth, because the purpose of the fight–flight response is to protect the organism, not to harm it. Although the negative interpretations are understandable, they contribute to a cycle of fear.

If the emergency response is activated in response to a threat that is obvious (such as a near accident or physical or verbal attack), the resulting emotional experience is different, because there is no fear of the fear. Fear of fear is described in the next section.

But How Does Panic Occur?

Until now, we have discussed the components of anxiety and panic and how these components may interact to spiral anxiety and panic. We have not discussed why the fight–flight response is activated when there is nothing to be frightened of. Why does the body go into emergency mode where there is no real danger?

Apparently, people with panic attacks are frightened by the physical sensations of the emergency response. In other words, panic attacks represent fear of fear. A panic attack follows a typical sequence. First, unexpected physical sensations are experienced. Second, fear is experienced.

The second part of this sequence is easy to understand. As discussed earlier, the emergency response causes the brain to search for danger. When an obvious external danger cannot be found, the mind looks inward and "invents" a reason, such as "I am dying or losing control." As noted earlier, if thoughts of illness are in the back of your mind anyway, you understandably focus on this danger. Obviously, such thoughts are fear provoking in and of themselves; anyone would feel afraid if she or he thought she or he was about to die or go crazy. Fear-provoking thoughts, in turn, intensify the fight–flight response, because the body reacts with an emergency response when danger arises. This response occurs even if the danger is based on a perception of what could happen. As a result, the very thing that is feared, that is, the physical sensations, is intensified as a result of the fear. Think of it—It is like being afraid of a dog, and the more afraid you became, the bigger the dog grew. In the case of panic attacks, a physical sensation is experienced, the sensation is feared; as a result, the sensation intensifies, and the fear intensifies. This spiraling lasts until the fear cycle is ended either by parasympathetic activation or by realizing that you no longer need to be afraid of the sensation (more about this part later). So, panic attacks are akin to phobias, but in this case, the phobic object is internal instead of external. By being afraid of a bodily sensation, the object of fear, that is, the sensation, can intensify, an effect that makes the fear different from other phobias. Another difference is that it is not always possible to predict when a physical sensation will occur, and it is not always possible to escape from a physical sensation. In contrast, an external phobic object, such as an animal, is usually predictable and escapable. Being afraid of something that is relatively unpredictable and inescapable creates a lot of anxiety about when it will recur and how to deal with it when it does recur.

In summary, panic attacks are generated by misinterpreting physical sensations as signs of impending death, craziness, loss of control, embarrassment, or fear of fear. After a number of times of being afraid of physical sensations, anxiety and fear can occur in response to the initial sensations without conscious thoughts of danger. That is, the fear of sensations occurs "automatically" without your consciously telling yourself anything. The "automatic" quality is typical of all interpretations; through repetition, the person begins to make associations without being fully aware of so doing. Similarly, behaviors can become automatic. Think of when you first learned to ride a bike or to drive. Initially, the activity took a lot of concentration and self-instruction about what to do each step of the way. Gradually it became automatic so that you can ride and drive without consciously thinking about what you are doing.

The automatic process of fearing bodily sensations can make panic attacks seem to occur from out of the blue. Although sometimes you may be aware of thoughts of danger, for example, "I'm having a heart attack," at other times you may not be aware of such thoughts. Instead, you just feel afraid.

There is a related automatic process called interoceptive conditioning. This process reflects learning to be afraid of physical sensations because of having negative experiences in association with those sensations. Of course, the trauma of panic attacks (particularly the first panics you ever had) meets the criteria of a negative experience. For example, it is like being burned every time you noticed your heart rate speeding up. Quickly, you would learn to be afraid of your heart speeding up in anticipation of being burned. When the feeling of panic becomes associated with a racing heart, changes in heart rate become feared in anticipation of terror. Then, even minor changes in heart rate that are normal and that did not bother you before you had experienced panic can elicit a fear response. In fact, the physical sensation may be so subtle that you are not fully aware of what triggered your panic attack.

Automatic misinterpretations of physical sensations and conditioned fear of sensations can make the attacks seem even more unpredictable and uncontrollable. Keep in mind that the sensations that trigger panic reactions and the negative misinterpretations of those sensations are always present, even if not immediately obvious.

The first part of the model is harder to understand. Why do you experience the physical symptoms of the emergency response if you are not frightened to begin with? There are many reasons for this reaction. One reason is stress. Stress from work pressures, relationships, or whatever can lead to an increase in the production of adrenaline and other chemicals that produce symptoms. This reaction is your body's way of staying alert and prepared to deal with the stress. However, one of the courses of action is the emergency fear response. Thus, stress alone can trigger an emergency response, especially in people who have experienced frightening or uncontrollable events earlier in life. Feeling stressed along with the chemical reaction of stress can thus set off the emergency response. This is particularly true if you are vulnerable to react to stress in this way, as we discussed earlier.

A second reason for experiencing sensations relates to anticipation of panic attacks. Anxious anticipation of anything contributes to higher levels of physical stress and hence more physical sensations of stress. Also, attention focuses on signals of the occurrence of whatever it is that one is anticipating. For example, anticipating a plane crash leads to an acute focus on noises or vibrations in a plane. In the case of panic, anxious anticipation of a panic attack increases arousal and symptomatology, as well as increasing vigilance for symptoms that are the signals of impending panic. That is, you may be scanning your body for unusual physical feelings and picking up on sensations you might not have otherwise noticed. In this way, anxious anticipation about panicking increases the likelihood of experiencing and noticing physical sensations. This, in turn, may be misinterpreted as being dangerous, and a panic attack results. Then, a cycle of anxious anticipation and panic attack begins.

There are several other reasons for experiencing physical sensations. Remember the discussion about interoceptive conditioning. Conditioning follows a principle called stimulus generalization, which means that stimuli that are similar to the primary stimulus can also elicit a learned fear reaction. An example is a fear of closed-in situations that a person developed after being locked in a small attic as a child. Through stimulus generalization, the fear could generalize to similar situations, such as elevators, tunnels, rest rooms, and small cars. Similarly, fears of emergency-response types of physical sensations can generalize to other sensations. For example, people with panic disorder are commonly fearful of caffeine; exercise; hot, humid weather conditions; anger and excitement; fatigue; and many other activities. All of these activities produce physical sensations similar to those experienced during panic.

Thus, the final model of panic attacks in a simplified way looks like the one in Figure 4.1.

As you read this model of panic, you may have some doubts, as did one of our clients, Jane. Here is how the therapist helped her to understand the explanation.

J: If I understand you correctly, you're saying that my panic attacks are the same as the fear I experienced the time we found a burglar in our house. But it doesn't feel the same at all.

T: Yes, those two emotional states—an unexpected panic attack and fear when confronted with a burglar—are essentially the same. However, in the case of the burglar, where were you focusing your attention—on the burglar or on the way you were feeling?

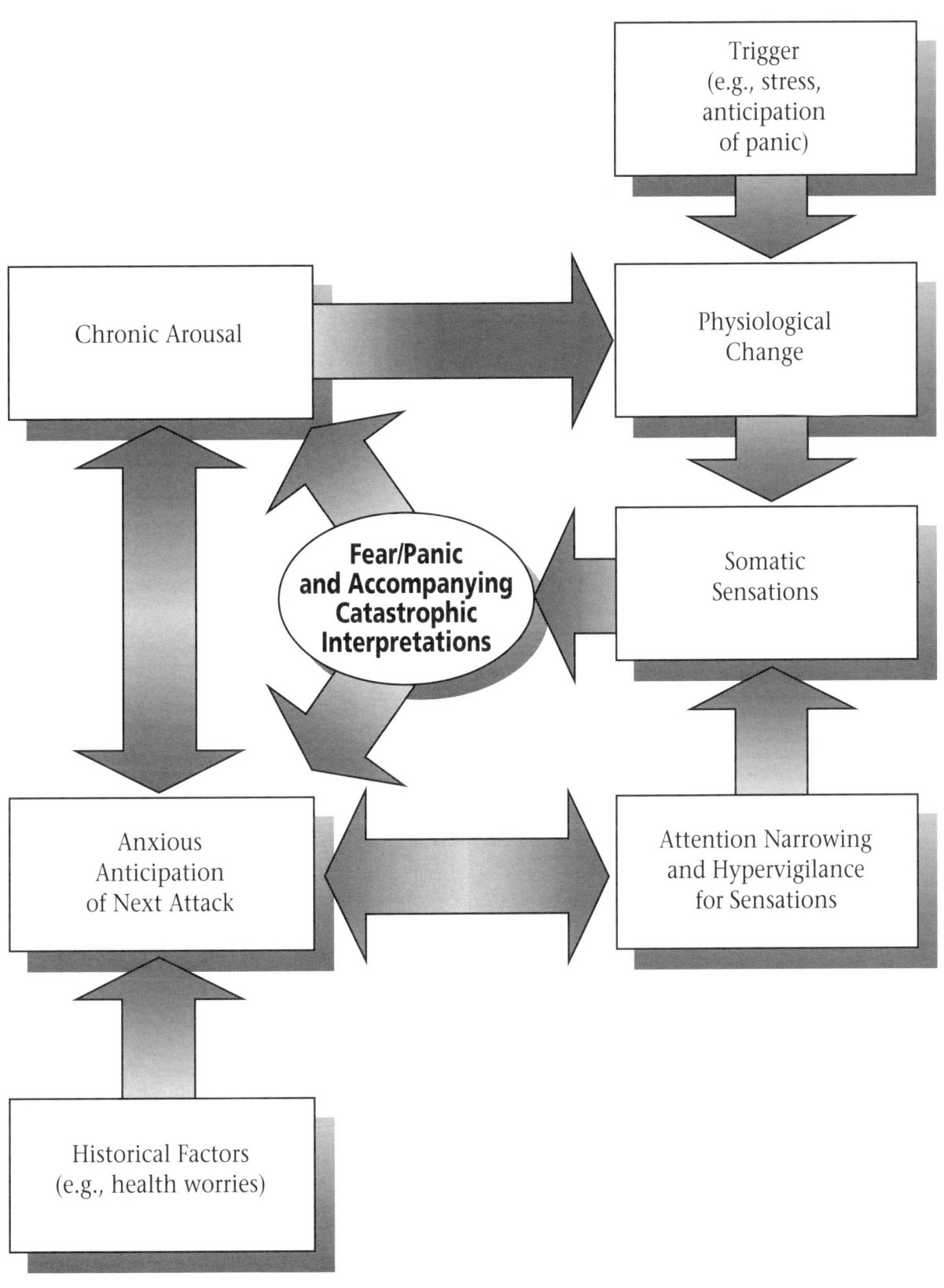

Figure 4.1. The Cycle of a Panic Attack

J: The burglar, of course, although I did notice that my heart was racing a mile a minute.

T: And when you have a panic attack, where are you focusing your attention—on the people around you or on the way you are feeling?

J: Well, mostly on the way I'm feeling, although it depends on where I am at the time.

T: All right, now being most concerned about what is going on inside you can lead to a very different type of experience than being concerned about a burglar, even though basically the same physiological response is occurring. For example, remember our description of the way in which fear of sensations can intensify the sensations.

J: Okay. But what about the feelings of unreality? You are saying that the symptoms I feel during a panic attack are actually protective. How can unreal feelings be protective, or how can feeling unreal help me deal with a dangerous situation?

T: Remember that it's the physiological events that are protective, and the sensations are the end result of those events. Now, feelings of unreality can be caused by changes in your blood flow to your brain, or from overbreathing, or from concentrating too intensely on what's going on inside you. So, the unreality sensation per se may not be protective, but the changes in blood flow and breathing are.

J: I understand that I can create a panic attack by being afraid of my bodily feelings, like my heart racing or feeling unreal. But sometimes it happens so quickly that I don't have time to think.

T: Yes, these reactions can occur very quickly, at times, automatically. But, remember, we are tuned to react instantly to things we think mean danger. Picture yourself walking through a jungle. Let's say that after a while, you are told that a lion has been seen nearby. Now your attention shifts dramatically to anything that suggests the possibility of a lion attack, such as noises in the bushes or branches moving. Well, the same thing happens with panic, but now what you pay attention to are bodily sensations.

In summary, then, panic is known as the emergency response because its primary purpose is to activate the organism and to protect it from harm. Everyone is capable of this response when confronted with danger. Associated with this response are a number of physical, behavioral, and mental changes. More important, once the danger has gone, many of these changes can continue, especially the physical ones, due to learning and other chronic arousal effects. When physical symptoms occur in the absence of an obvious explanation, people often misinterpret the normal emergency symptoms as indicating a serious physical or mental problem. In this case, the sensations themselves can become threatening and can trigger the emergency response again. It is, therefore, important to recognize certain myths and misinterpretations about the emergency response and to know the most common ones. Although we discuss these myths in more detail later as they relate to your own panic reaction, here is a review of some of the most common ones.

Common Myths

Going Crazy

Many people believe that when they experience the physical symptoms of the emergency response, they are going crazy. They are most likely referring to the severe mental disorder known as schizophrenia. Let us look at schizophrenia to see how likely this is. Schizophrenia is a major disorder characterized by severe symptoms. These symptoms can include disjointed thoughts and speech, sometimes extending to nonsensical speech; delusions or strange beliefs; and hallucinations. For example, a strange belief is the receiving of messages from outer space; an hallucination is hearing voices that are not really there.

Schizophrenia generally begins very gradually, not suddenly such as during a panic. Additionally, because it runs strongly in families and has a genetic base, only a certain proportion of people can become schizophrenic; in other people, no amount of stress will cause the disorder. A third important point is that people who become schizophrenic usually show some mild symptoms for most of their lives (such as unusual thoughts, flowery speech, etc.). Thus, if you have not experienced such symptoms, then the chances are that you will not become schizophrenic. This is especially true if you are over 25 years of age since schizophrenia generally first appears in the late teens to early twenties. Finally, if you have been through interviews with a psychologist or psychiatrist, then you can be fairly certain that you would know by now if you are likely to become schizophrenic.

Losing Control

Some people believe they are going to lose control when they panic. Presumably, they mean that they will become totally paralyzed and not be able to move or that they will not know what they are doing and will run around wild, hurting people or yelling out obscenities and embarrassing themselves. Alternatively, they

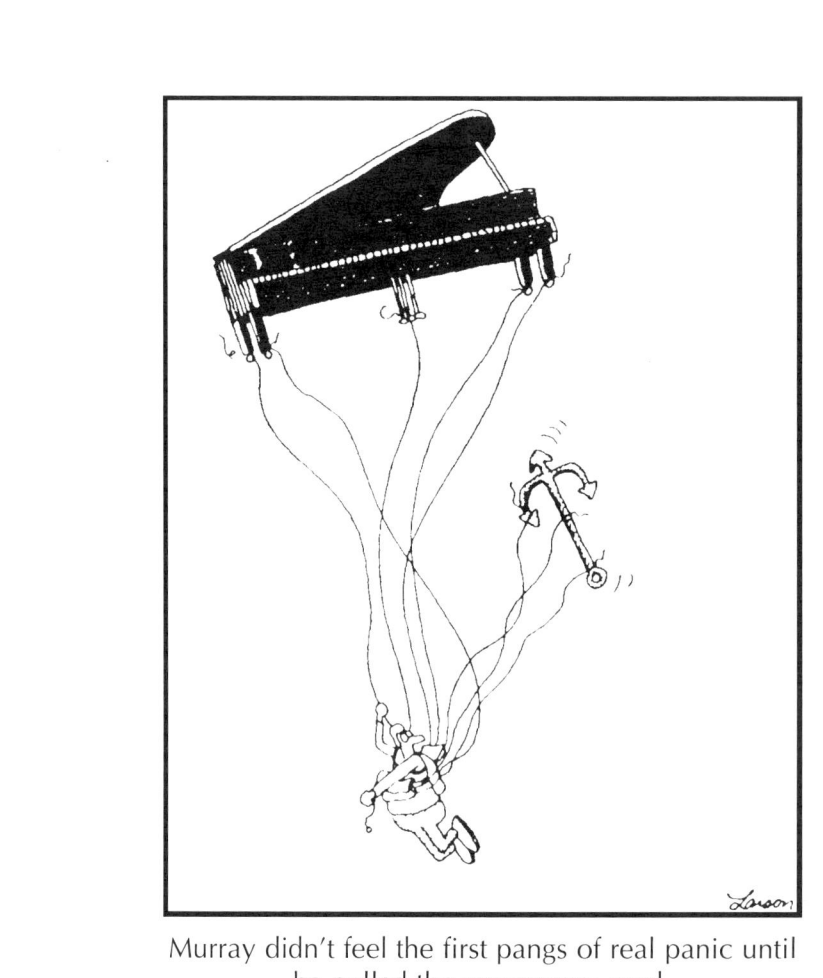

Murray didn't feel the first pangs of real panic until he pulled the emergency cord.

may not know what to expect but may just experience an overwhelming feeling that something bad is going to happen.

From our earlier discussion, you know where this feeling comes from. During the emergency response, the entire body is ready for action and there is an overwhelming desire to escape. However, the emergency response is not aimed at hurting people who are not a threat, and it will not produce paralysis. Rather, the entire response is designed to get you away from potential danger. There has never been a recorded case of someone going "wild" during a panic. Even though the emergency response can make you feel somewhat confused, and unreal, especially if there is no real external source of threat, you are still able to think and function normally. Ironically, if you are using the response, you are able to think faster and more clearly, you are actually physically stronger, and your reflexes are quicker. For example, think of mothers who accomplish amazing feats and overcome intense fears when their children are in danger.

Sometimes, the strong drive to escape is misperceived as losing control. That is, the person thinks, "Because I do everything I can to get out or get help, then I really must be crazy." For example, one patient was very fearful of losing control. Her concern was based on the fact that on one occasion when driving to a job interview she panicked, changed direction, and drove to her husband's office instead. She perceived these actions as loss of control because she felt anxious when she did not want to feel anxious and because she felt the strong urge to be with her husband even though at some level she realized that this was not necessary. On the contrary, she was in complete control—She was functioning to escape the situation of being alone and was directing her behavior toward that escape. Given her fears of the moment, which were identified as being fearful of permanent feelings of unreality, getting to her husband was natural and helpful. Most people would do the same if they believed they were about to slip into a state of permanent unreality. So, the behavior was controlled—The problem lies in the fears of unreality.

Nervous Collapse

Many people are frightened by beliefs that their nerves might become exhausted and they may collapse. As discussed earlier, the emergency response is produced through activity in the sympathetic nervous system, which is counteracted by the parasympathetic nervous system. The parasympathetic nervous system is, in a sense, a safeguard to protect against the possibility that the sympathetic nervous system may become "worn out." Nerves are not like electrical wires, and anxiety cannot wear out, damage, or use up nerves. The worst that can happen during a panic attack is that an individual faints, at which point the sympathetic nervous system stops its overactivity and the person regains consciousness within a few seconds. However, actually passing out as a result of the emergency response is quite rare. If it does occur, it is important because it is a way for the body to return to normal. Another concern is that repeated panic and anxiety increase the chances of future nervous collapse. Again, anxiety does not physically wear out nerves. On the contrary, there is even some evidence to suggest that by repeated experiences of stress and anxiety you may toughen or strengthen your nervous system. For example, in times of severe national crisis or disaster such as war, the incidence of psychological problems does not increase, but, instead, there seems to be a "toughening up" to deal with the stress.

Heart Attacks

Many people misinterpret the symptoms of the emergency response as signs of heart attack, probably because they do not have enough knowledge about heart attacks. The symptoms of heart disease differ from those of panic attacks. The major symptoms of heart disease are breathlessness and chest pain, as well as occasional palpitations and fainting. Generally, the symptoms of heart disease are directly related to effort. That is, the harder you exercise, the worse the symptoms become, and the less you exercise, the better the symptoms become. Heart disease symptoms usually go away fairly quickly with rest. This is very different from the symptoms associated with panic attacks, which often occur at rest and seem to have a "mind" of their own. Certainly, panic symptoms can occur during exercise or can intensify during exercise. This is different from the symptoms of a heart attack because they can occur equally often at rest. Of most importance, heart disease will almost always produce major electrical changes in the heart, which are detected by an electrocardiogram (EKG) recording. In panic attacks, the only change that shows up on an EKG is an increase in heart rate. Thus, if you have had an EKG and the doctor has given you the "all clear," you can safely assume that heart disease is not the cause of your attacks.

A related misconception is that repeated panic attacks increase the risk of heart attacks or other dangerous physical conditions later on. Although there is evidence to suggest that chronic stress and strain increase the risk of cardiovascular or cerebral diseases as a person ages, chronic stress and strain are very different from panic attacks. As you know by now, panic attacks are short bursts of adrenaline and arousal, similar in many ways to the type of arousal that would occur during physical exercise. There is no evidence that panic attacks in themselves have cumulative health risks. However, chronic anxiety about having panic attacks may increase the risk of later physical problems. This is more reason to realize that panic attacks are harmless surges of emotions, so that you no longer chronically anticipate their recurrence. Furthermore, although chronic anxiety may increase the risk of later disease, the degree to which risk is increased is not in any way as great as that due to poor lifestyle factors (such as a fatty diet, lack of exercise, smoking, and substance abuse).

Fainting

Fear of fainting is common in people with panic disorder. The fear of fainting is usually based on a misinterpretation of symptoms such as dizziness and lightheadedness as precursors to fainting. In fact, fainting is rare during panic attacks because the state of panic is incompatible with fainting. This is because the speeding up of the autonomic nervous system, that is, the heart rate, during a panic attack is the direct opposite of the slowing down of the autonomic nervous system during fainting. Fainting is most likely in people who have low blood pressure or who respond to stress with major reductions in blood pressure. Finally, as mentioned before, if fainting does occur it is an adaptive or useful mechanism that allows the body to return to a normal level of functioning.

Other common myths about panics include aneurysm, epilepsy and death from shock.

Summary

Think of any other major fears that you have in relation to panic attacks. Sometimes it is difficult to identify these thoughts because they become almost habitual. If you are frightened of the feeling of panic, ask yourself why, or what negative things you think could happen if you panic. You will be working through these questions in more detail in the following chapters but start to ask yourself those questions now. Do you hold any of the myths that are described in this chapter? If you do, despite evidence to suggest that they are not accurate, imagine how those beliefs contribute to the spiral of fear.

It is important to understand where misinterpretations originate. People tend to look for an external cause for the sense of danger, and when that cause is not apparent, it seems logical to look internally and to attribute the panic to some physical or mental problem. The specific content of the attribution can be influenced by information given to you from other people. For example, we have come across a dictionary definition of panic (in a reputable medical guide) as "a state that can lead into psychotic depression." That is misinformation. There is no evidence to suggest that panic leads to psychosis. However, for someone without a background in psychological research, that kind of information can easily provide the basis for a fear of becoming psychotic during panic attacks. If someone is afraid of becoming psychotic, then it is understandable that the experience of panic is terrifying and leads to anxiety about the next panic attack.

Exercise

The information in this chapter may be very different from the kind of understanding that you had previously. Therefore, it is essential that you read through this material several times before beginning the next lesson. Allow yourself time to integrate the information thoroughly, to understand what panic is and the basis for the physiological reactions that occur during panic. In addition, as you do your monitoring over the week, using your Daily Mood Record and Panic Attack Record, keep a close watch on the kinds of thoughts you have related to either the anticipation or the experience of panic. Allow yourself a full week of integrating this lesson's information and understanding your anxiety and panic before continuing with the next lesson.

Self-Assessment

Answer by circling **T** (True) or **F** (False). Answers are provided in Appendix A.

1. A panic attack is a medical problem over which you have no control. **T F**

2. The symptoms experienced during panic, such as racing heart and sweating, indicate a physical disease process that is dangerous. **T F**

3. Panic is an emergency response that is primarily a protective mechanism.   T   F

4. Panics that seem to occur from out of the blue often can be related to subtle events such as changes in breathing patterns or excitement from other events.   T   F

5. When the body is activated into a panic reaction, it could go on forever and ever.   T   F

6. People do not go crazy when they panic.   T   F

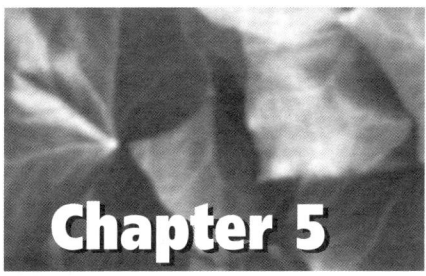

Chapter 5

Learning Physical Control

Review

Examine your Panic Attack Record and Daily Mood Record from the past week. Have any further patterns emerged from your monitoring? Have your panic attacks become more understandable in terms of the sequence of thoughts, behaviors, and sensations that spiral into fear? Have you been able to identify patterns of thoughts that feed into the panic cycle? Have you noticed situations or activities that you avoid because of the anticipation of panic? Add your monitoring data (average anxiety and number of panic attacks over the past week) to your Progress Record.

Control of Physical Sensations

In this session you will learn a method of controlling some of the fear-provoking physical sensations. The first set of sensations addressed are related to breathing. Studies have shown that 50%–60% of people who panic show some signs of overbreathing or hyperventilation. Overbreathing is involved in panic attacks in two ways. First, overbreathing may produce an initial sensation that frightens you and leads to a panic attack. Second, overbreathing can develop as part of the panic reaction after the fear has begun. You need to decide whether overbreathing is an important part of your panics. If it is not, deep relaxation might be used as an alternative method of controlling your physical sensations. This method is discussed later in this chapter. There are several ways of determining whether hyperventilating is part of your panics. First, answer the following questions:

1. In general, do you often feel short of breath, as if you are not getting enough air?

2. Do you sometimes feel as if you are suffocating?

3. Do you experience chest pain, tingling, prickling, and numbness sensations?

4. Do you yawn or sigh a lot or take in big gulps of air?

5. When you are frightened, do you hold your breath or breathe quickly and shallowly?

If you answered yes to any of these questions, then it is likely that overbreathing plays a part in your panic reactions. Of course, if you are like many people, you may not be aware of your breathing patterns. Therefore, it is important to test yourself.

Try a short exercise. Sit in a comfortable chair and breathe very fast and very deep, as though you are blowing up a balloon. Try to continue for a minute and a half. When doing this exercise, it is important that you exhale very hard and take the air very deeply into your lungs. Be very forceful and deep in your breathing. Once you have finished the exercise, close your eyes and breathe slowly, pausing at the end of each breath. Continue the slow breathing for 1–2 minutes, until the sensations have passed. Now, think about the sensations you experienced. Check off the sensations on one of your Panic Attack Records. Did you experience symptoms similar to those experienced when you panic? Possibly you might not have been as fearful as you might have been had the same symptoms occurred at another time, because you have an obvious explanation for these sensations. Nevertheless, were the physical sensations similar to the sensations you experience during naturally occurring panic attacks?

A big overlap between the effects of hyperventilation and your natural panic attacks is a good indicator that overbreathing plays a role in your panic attacks. If the symptoms were not similar, try the overbreathing procedure again, but this time continue for 2–2 minutes. At the end, again assess whether the sensations were similar to those that you experience naturally. If not, then it is likely that overbreathing is not significant to your panics. In that case, relaxation techniques may be more helpful, so you may skip the next section and proceed to relaxation training. On the other hand, if the sensations produced by hyperventilating were similar to your natural panic sensations, continue with this section for breathing retraining.

Some people find that they get something out of both breathing retraining and relaxation. There is certainly nothing wrong with doing both. However, the worst thing you could do is to try each exercise halfheartedly. Whether you do one or both, you must put in your full effort to get the benefits.

Breathing Physiology

Before learning the correct method of breathing, you must understand the physiology of overbreathing. The body needs oxygen to survive. When you inhale, oxygen is taken into the lungs where it is picked up by the hemoglobin (the "oxygen sticky" chemical in the blood). The hemoglobin carries the oxygen around the body where it is released for use by the cells. The cells use the oxygen in their energy reactions, producing a by-product called carbon dioxide (CO_2), which, in turn, is released back into the blood, transported to the lungs, and exhaled.

Efficient control of the body's energy reactions depends on a balance between oxygen and CO_2. This balance is maintained chiefly through the rate and depth of breathing. Breathing too much will increase levels of oxygen in the blood and decrease levels of CO_2, because the oxygen is not used at the same rate that it is taken in. Breathing too little will decrease levels of oxygen and increase levels of CO_2. The appropriate rate of breathing, at rest, is about 10–14 breaths per minute.

Hyperventilation is defined as a rate and depth of breathing that is too much for the body's needs at a given time. If the need for oxygen and the production of CO_2 both increase (such as during exercise), breathing rates will increase. Alternatively, if the need for oxygen and the production of CO_2 both decrease (such as during relaxation), breathing rates will decrease.

Although most of the body's mechanisms, including breathing, are controlled by "automatic" chemical and physical means, breathing may also be put under voluntary control. For example, humans can quite easily hold their breath when swimming or speed up their breathing when blowing up a balloon. Therefore, a number of "nonautomatic" factors, such as emotion, stress, or habit, can cause humans to change their breathing. These factors may be especially important in people who have panic attacks.

Interestingly, although most people consider oxygen to be the determining factor in breathing, the body uses CO_2 as its "marker" for breathing rates. The most important effect of overbreathing is to produce a marked drop in CO_2. This drop, in turn, produces a drop in the acid content of the blood and leads to what is known as alkaline blood. It is these two effects—a decrease in blood CO_2 content and an increase in blood alkalinity—that are responsible for most of the physical changes that occur during overbreathing.

One of the most important changes produced by hyperventilation is a narrowing of certain blood vessels in the body. In particular, the blood flow to the brain is somewhat decreased. Together with the tightening of blood vessels, the hemoglobin increases its "stickiness" for oxygen. Thus, not only does less blood reach certain areas of the body, but the oxygen carried by the blood is less likely to be released to the tissues. Paradoxically, although overbreathing means a person is taking in more oxygen, he or she is actually getting less oxygen to certain areas of the brain and body. This results in two broad categories of symptoms: (a) centrally, symptoms are produced by the slight reduction in oxygen to certain parts of the brain, including dizziness, lightheadedness, confusion, breathlessness, blurred vision, and unreality. (b) Peripherally, some symptoms are produced by the slight reduction in oxygen to certain parts of the body, including an increase in heart rate to pump more blood around; numbness and tingling in the extremities; cold, clammy hands; and muscle stiffness.

The reductions in oxygen are slight and totally harmless. Also, overbreathing (possibly due to a reduction in oxygen to the brain) can produce feelings of breathlessness, choking, or smothering, so a person feels as if she or he is not getting enough air. However, this feeling is in contrast to what is actually happening.

Overbreathing is also responsible for a number of overall effects. First, the act of overbreathing is hard physical work, and it often produces a feeling of being hot, flushed, and sweaty. Second, because it is hard work to overbreathe, prolonged periods of overbreathing will often result in tiredness and exhaustion. Third, people who overbreathe often tend to breathe from their chest rather than from their diaphragm (the muscle underneath the lungs, central to the base of the rib cage). Chest breathing tends to make chest muscles tired and tense and leads to chest pressure and tightness or even chest pain. Finally, many people who overbreathe tend to repeatedly sigh or yawn. These patterns are actually forms of hyperventilation, because whenever a person yawns or sighs, a large quantity of CO_2 is "dumped" quickly. Therefore, it is important to become aware of habitual sighing and yawning and to try to suppress these habits.

You might experience many of the overbreathing symptoms but without seeming to hyperventilate. That is, you may not think that you gasp for air or breathe very quickly. However, hyperventilation can be very subtle, especially if it has been a pattern over a long period of time. During chronic overbreathing, there can be marked drops in CO_2 but, due to compensation in the body, relatively little change in alkalinity occurs. The compensation lessens the chances of acute symptoms. However, because CO_2 levels are kept low, the body loses some of its ability to cope with changes in CO_2, so even a slight change in breathing, such as a yawn, can trigger symptoms. In fact, the vulnerability to changes in breathing may be one reason for panic attacks that seem to occur from out of the blue. If you are not aware of the initial breathing symptom trigger, then the resulting panic attack may seem to be spontaneous.

Probably the most important point to be made about hyperventilation is that it is not dangerous. In fact, forced hyperventilation is a common medical test. Breathing patterns are an integral part of the emergency response and are intended to protect the body from danger. The changes associated with hyperventilating are those that prepare the body for action in order to escape harm, as noted earlier. If fleeing or fighting actually occurred, a state of overbreathing would not develop because the oxygen would be used at the rate it is taken in. However, hyperventilating is not dangerous. It is understandable though for the brain to expect danger and for the individual to feel the urge to escape once acute hyperventilation has begun.

Sometimes people are concerned that if they overbreathe for too long, eventually they will either collapse or faint, or some other negative event will happen. In fact, as just described, natural bodily mechanisms come in to play to adjust for chronic overbreathing so that it is not dangerous. Similarly, sometimes people are concerned that overbreathing will lead to fainting or seizure. Fainting almost never occurs as a result of overbreathing. When it does, it tends to occur in people who have an actual history of fainting. That is, they have some other feature in their makeup that makes them more likely to faint. The same is true for seizures. Overbreathing alone almost never induces a seizure, unless the person is already vulnerable to seizures for other reasons.

Breathing Control Procedures

Once you fully understand the reasons and basis of overbreathing, the next step is to learn breathing retraining. This is a skill and therefore takes practice. The reasons for breathing retraining are (a) to decrease some of the physical cues to which you are very sensitive (i.e., the initial triggers for panic attacks), (b) to reduce physical sensations during panics, and (c) to facilitate general relaxation, which will reduce levels of tension and, therefore, impede the cycle of panic.

The exercise we have found to be best involves two components. The first is slowing your breathing. You must learn to think about your breathing while you breathe smoothly and normally. This is difficult for many people, and you may find that when you start to think about and count your breathing, it speeds up. This is due to sensitivity to symptoms of overbreathing; because the symptoms have been associated with panic, they have become cues or signals of which you are afraid. Once you can think about your breathing, while maintaining a normal rate and depth, then you can begin to slow it down.

The second component is a meditational one that helps you to strengthen your attention. Attention is very much like a muscle, and requires constant exercise to stay strong. Good attention is important because it will help you to concentrate on your breathing when you become anxious or panicky.

The First Breathing Control Exercise

The following exercise is to be practiced two times every day for a minimum of 10 minutes each time. We recommend that you practice this exercise over the next week (7 days). If the exercise is difficult at first, do not stop. It will become easier with practice. Find a quiet, comfortable place where you will not be disturbed. Once you become good at controlling your breathing, you will be asked to practice anywhere at any time. Initially though, it is best to practice in a quiet, comfortable area.

Sit in a comfortable chair and allow yourself a few seconds to calm down. Start to *count* on your in-breaths. That is, when you breathe in, think *one* to yourself. As you breathe out, think the word *relax*. Think *two* on the next breath in and *relax* on the next breath out. Continue up to *ten* and then back down to *one*.

Ideally, you should think of nothing but your breathing and the words. This is very difficult for some people, and you may never be able to do it perfectly. When you begin to do this exercise, you may not get past the first number without other thoughts coming into your mind. This is natural. When this happens, do not get angry or give up. Simply allow the thoughts to pass through your mind and bring your attention back to the numbers. You may have to practice this many times before you reach number two.

At first, while you count each breath, breathe at your *usual rate and depth*. Do not take in too much air and do not try to slow your breathing just yet. Just breathe smoothly and easily. To help yourself do this, place one hand on your chest and the other hand on your stomach with the little finger about 1 inch above the navel. Movement should come almost entirely from the lower (stomach) hand. Try to prevent the chest area from moving. If you are an habitual chest breather, this kind of breathing may feel artificial and cause feelings of breathlessness. That is a natural response—Just remember that you are indeed getting enough oxygen and the feelings of breathlessness will lessen the more you practice. If you find it extremely difficult to keep your chest still, lie down on the floor, flat on your stomach, with your hands clasped under your head. This position will make it easier to breathe from the diaphragm. Once you have done this exercise several times and feel comfortable breathing from the diaphragm, turn over and put a book on your stomach. Then, as you breathe in, try to raise the book. That is, every breath in should be accompanied by a ballooning out of the diaphragm, and every breath out should be accompanied by pulling in of the diaphragm. Try to keep your breathing *smooth* and fluid. Do not gulp in a big breath and then let it out all at once. Also, breathe through your nose. Breathing through the nose makes it more likely that you will breathe out slowly. It is not essential that you breathe through your nose, but if you breathe through your mouth, try to keep the opening small so that you exhale slowly.

Now try the exercise described earlier in which you count up to *ten* and back to *one*.

Now that you have done the exercise, evaluate how it went. Did you feel breathless or a little dizzy or did your breathing speed up as you began? If you felt intense sensations, you can stop the exercise for a while, calm down, and then begin again. Your reaction is just an indication of your sensitivity to the sensations associated with breathing. As you continue to do the exercise, the reactivity will diminish. Was it difficult for you to take in a breath deeply, down to the diaphragm? If so, try to push your stomach out just before you breathe in so that there is space for the air to fill. Remember, however, not to take in more than your usual amount of air. Also remember to think of the air as oozing and escaping from your nose rather than being suddenly released when you exhale.

Practice this exercise every day two times a day for at least 10 minutes each time, over the next week. Do not try to slow your breathing yet. Overall, it is most important that you practice regularly. If results are not immediate, do not despair. Remember that with this technique you are (a) learning to reduce sensations that may trigger panic attacks and (b) learning to reduce overbreathing that occurs as part of fear and panic.

At this point, you should not try to use this technique in specific situations or when you become frightened. Trying to use a strategy that is only partially developed can be more frustrating and anxiety producing than not trying it at all. A parallel example is teaching scuba divers a method of dealing with underwater crises once and expecting them to use the procedure in an actual emergency. Instead, scuba divers must practice the emergency procedure over and over again before going deep underwater so that emergency procedures become automatic and, therefore, may be used at times of real emergency. So, begin by learning to feel comfortable using the technique by practicing in a quiet, comfortable environment. An outline of the exercise is provided below.

Outline for Breathing Retraining: Stage 1

Step	Description
1	Comfortable, quiet location.
2	Count one on breath in and think relax on breath out.
3	Focus attention on breathing and counting.
4	Normal rate and depth of breathing.
5	Expand diaphragm on breath in and keep chest still.
6	Count up to ten and back to one.
7	Practice two times per day, 10 minutes each time, for 7 days.
8	Monitor your practice.

After each practice, monitor your levels of concentration on the breathing exercise and ease of breathing, using the Breathing Retraining Record. An example is shown in Figure 5.1. Each form should last one week and there are enough forms

Breathing Retraining Record
If doing relaxation training ONLY, see other side.

See Figure 5.1 in your workbook.

```
0     1     2     3     4     5     6     7     8
None        Mild        Moderate    Strong      Extreme
```

For each practice, rate your concentration and ease of breathing according to the scale above.

Date	Practice	Concentration during the exercise	Ease of breathing
3/01	1	0	1
3/01	2	1	1
3/02	1	1	2
3/02	2	0	1
3/03	1	1	2
3/03	2	2	3
3/04	1	2	3
3/04	2	3	3
3/05	1	4	3
3/05	2	2	3
3/06	1	5	5
3/06	2	5	4
3/07	1	5	5
3/07	2	5	5

Copyright © 1994 Graywind Publications, Inc.   Mastery of Your Anxiety and Panic

Figure 5.1. Example of Breathing Retraining Record

for the entire program in your MAP–II Monitoring Forms packet. These will provide feedback for you and your doctor or mental health professional.

Muscle Relaxation Training

Tensing of the muscles is another component of anxiety and panic. Muscle tension has survival value because it is a necessary step in preparing for action. It is difficult to run or fight off danger when you are relaxed. Muscle tension is also part of the general state of alertness and vigilance that characterizes general anxiety.

Try this exercise. For 1 minute, tense your body as much as you can without causing pain. Tense your legs, your arms, your face, your shoulders, your back, your stomach—Tense everything. What are the effects of that kind of tension? It may produce sensations including tremor and shaking, weakness, pain in different parts of your body, fatigue, stiffening of the muscles, neck stiffness, tenderness around the head, or a feeling of being immobilized. Constant tension can produce headaches, extreme tiredness, and other muscle aches and pains. Assess whether the sensations you just felt are similar to those you feel when anxious or panicky.

Muscle tension can produce a range of sensations that can become frightening because they have been associated with anxiety or fear in the past. Because a strong connection exists between physical tension and a feeling of fear, it is understandable that awareness of muscle tension can produce feelings of being in danger, even if none exists. Tension is part of the body's preparation for action, but if action does not take place, the residual symptoms are much more noticeable.

The exercise we find most helpful for reducing tension is called progressive muscle relaxation. This is a technique developed by a doctor named Jacobson and has since proven very effective. It entails releasing tension from major muscle groups in your body and concentrating on the experience in an objective way.

Sometimes, people with panic disorder are frightened by deep relaxation. Fear of relaxation can occur because of the sense of losing control. By truly relaxing, a person lets his or her guard down, and for someone who fears harmful or dangerous things at all times, the relaxation becomes anxiety provoking. Learning that you are safe even though you are relaxed, that is, continuing with the relaxation exercises and realizing that nothing bad happens, is the best way of overcoming fear of loss of control during relaxation. In addition, fear of relaxation can occur because deep relaxation can produce frightening feelings, such as sensations of floating, dizziness, heaviness, or weakness. Relaxation-induced sensations might then act in the same way as do other physical sensations that you have associated with panic attacks; that is, they become triggers for panic. If that happens, analyze it and appreciate that this is an example of your sensitivity that is out of proportion to any real danger. As we discuss later, the primary method of getting over that sensitivity is repeated, controlled exposure. In other words, feeling frightened at first by the relaxation is an indication that the most important thing for you to do is to continue with the procedure. The more you do it, the less uneasy and more relaxed you will feel.

Initially, the procedure takes about half an hour because you work through 16 major muscle groups. However, once you have become skilled in the method, the procedure is progressively shortened because you focus on 8 muscle groups, then 4 muscle groups, and finally one-step relaxation.

The exercise entails tensing of the muscles followed by release or relaxation. The tensing has two purposes. First, the tension–relaxation mechanism is like a pendulum; the farther you pull it one way, the farther it will go the other when released. The more tension you produce, the more easily you can relax. Second, purposeful tension lets you become aware of the differences in sensations produced by tension versus those produced by relaxation. This awareness will allow you to detect tension even at mild levels. Then, you will be in a better position to use the relaxation technique as soon as you are aware of tension, instead of waiting for it to build to high levels.

It is important to concentrate on sensations in each part of your body during the exercise. It is easy for other thoughts to come into your mind. Try to let them pass through. Do not focus on them, and do not get angry or frustrated by them and give up. Just return your attention to the relaxation.

Begin by practicing the exercise in a quiet environment. Later, it will be important to practice in distracting environments so that you can apply this skill wherever you are when anxious. Concentration is important because, wherever you are, being able to focus on relaxing is essential to the effectiveness of this procedure. Find a quiet place and a comfortable chair that provides support for your neck. If you do not have a comfortable, high-back chair, lie on your bed, but do not fall asleep. Relaxation is indeed a useful technique for people who have problems going to sleep, but, in this case, you are learning a method of control to be applied in daily life. It is not reasonable to fall asleep when you begin to feel anxious in a shopping mall. Make sure that there are no pressure points on your body as you practice. That is, do not have your legs or arms crossed, and loosen tight shoes, belts, or clothing. Do not practice relaxation when you feel pressure to be doing something else, like chores. Devote a certain time every day just to the relaxation. Feeling that there are other things you should be doing is bound to create tension.

This exercise should be practiced every day two times a day for the next 7 days. Initially, that means 30 minutes twice a day. This practice is necessary to benefit from the procedure because, as with the other techniques discussed, relaxation is a skill that requires practice. Do not expect major changes initially. With practice, you will feel the effects of the relaxation.

Now, read the following set of instructions very carefully. Then, if possible, record the instructions to yourself on a tape. Find a comfortable position and play the tape back to yourself and follow the instructions. As you become familiar with the procedures, the tape will not be necessary, and you can practice without it.

Get into a comfortable position, close your eyes, and just sit quietly for a few seconds.

1. First, build up the tension in the lower arms by making fists with your hands and pulling up on the wrists. Feel the tension through the lower arms, the wrists, the fingers, the knuckles, and the hands. Focus on the tension—Notice the sensations of pulling, of discomfort, of tightness. Hold the tension for 10 seconds. Now, release the tension, and let your hands and lower arms relax beside you on the chair or bed, with the palms facing down. Focus your attention onto the sensations in your hands and arms. Feel the release from tension. (Relax the muscles for 20 seconds.)

2. Now, build up the tension in the upper arms by pulling the arms back and in toward your sides. Try not to tense muscles in other parts of your body although there will be some overlap. Feel the tension in the back of the arms radiating up into the shoulders and into your back. Focus on the sensations of tension. Hold the tension (10 seconds). Now, release the arms and let them relax heavily down. Focus on your upper arms and feel the difference in comparison to the tension. Your arms might feel heavy, warm, and relaxed. (Relax for 20 seconds.)

3. Now, build up the tension in the lower legs by flexing your feet and pulling your toes toward your upper body. Feel the tension as it spreads through your feet, your ankles, your shins, and your calves. Feel the tension spreading down the back of the legs into the feet, under the foot and around the toes. Focus on that part of your body (10 seconds). Now, release the leg tension. Let your legs relax onto the chair or the bed. Feel the difference in the muscles as they relax. Feel the release from tension, the sense of comfort, the warmth and heaviness of relaxation. (Relax for 20 seconds.)

4. Now, build up the tension in the upper legs by pulling the knees together and lifting the legs off the bed or chair. Focus on the tightness through the upper legs. Feel the pulling sensations from the hip down and notice the tension in the legs. Focus on that part of your body (10 seconds). Now, release the tension, and let the legs drop heavily down onto the chair or bed. Let the tension disappear. Focus on the feeling of relaxation. Feel the difference in your legs. Focus on the sense of comfort (20 seconds).

5. Now, build up the tension in your stomach by pulling your stomach in toward the spine, very tight. Feel the tension. Feel the tightness and focus on that part of your body (10 seconds). Now let the stomach go—Let it go farther and farther. Feel the sense of warmth circulating across your stomach. Feel the comfort of relaxation. (For 20 seconds, focus on that part of your body.)

6. Now, build up the tension around your chest by taking in a deep breath and holding it. Your chest is expanded, and the muscles are stretched around your chest—Feel the tension around your front and your back. Hold your breath (10 seconds). Now, slowly let the air escape and resume normal breathing, letting the air flow in and out smoothly and easily. Feel the difference as the muscles relax in comparison to the tension.

7. Now, for the shoulders, imagine they are on strings being pulled up toward your ears. Feel the tension around your shoulders, radiating down into your back and up into your neck and the back of your head. Focus on that part of your body. Describe the sensations to yourself. Focus (10 seconds) and then let the shoulders droop down. Let them droop farther and farther, feeling very relaxed. Feel the sense of relaxation in that part of your body. Focus on the comfort of relaxation (20 seconds).

8. Build up the tension around your neck by pressing the back of your neck toward the chair or bed and pulling your chin down toward your chest. Feel the tightness around the back of the neck and up into your head. Focus on the tension (10 seconds). Now release, letting your head rest heavily against the bed or chair. Nothing is holding it up except the support behind. Focus on the relaxation (20 seconds) and feel the difference from the tension.

9. Build up the tension around your mouth and jaw and throat by clenching your teeth and forcing the corners of your mouth back into a forced smile. Hold the tension (10 seconds). Feel the tightness in that part of your body. Describe the sensations to yourself. Now release the tension, letting the mouth drop down and the muscles around the throat and jaw relax. Focus on the difference in the sensations in that part of your body (20 seconds).

10. Now, build up the tension around your eyes by squeezing your eyes tightly together for a few seconds and release. Let the tension disappear from around your eyes. Feel the difference as the muscles relax.

"Listen... You've got to relax... The more you think about changing colors, the less chance you'll succeed... Shall we try the green background again?"

11. Now, build up the tension across the lower forehead by frowning and by pulling your eyebrows down and toward the center. Feel the tension across your forehead and across the top of your head. Focus on the tension (10 seconds) and then release, smoothing out the wrinkles and letting the forehead relax. Feel the difference in the sensations.

12. Finally, build up the tension in the upper forehead by raising your eyebrows as high as you can. Feel the wrinkling and the pulling sensations across the forehead and the across top of the head. Hold the tension (10 seconds) and then relax, letting the eyebrows back down and the tension from your forehead leave. Focus on the sensation of relaxation. Feel the difference in comparison to the tension.

Now your whole body is feeling relaxed and comfortable. Counting from one to five, feel yourself becoming even more relaxed, even further relaxed. One, letting all the tension leave your body. Two, sinking further and further into relaxation. Three, feeling more and more relaxed. Four, feeling very relaxed. Five, feeling deeply relaxed. Now, as you spend a few minutes in this relaxed state, think about your breathing. Feel the cool air as you breathe in and the warm air as you breathe out. Your breathing is slow and regular. And, every time you breathe out, think to yourself the word relax . . . relax . . . relax. Feeling comfortable and relaxed. . . . (continue for about 1–2 minutes). Now, counting backward from five to one, gradually feel yourself becoming more alert and awake. Five, feeling more awake. Four, coming out of the relaxation. Three, feeling more alert. Two, opening your eyes. One, sitting up.

This completes the instructions for muscle relaxations. Stop recording for the tape here. Once you learn this procedure, you might lower your heart rate and blood pressure while relaxing. For that reason, it is a good idea not to stand quickly after relaxing.

Now, practice the exercise.

Assess your experience. Were there any particular parts of your body that were difficult to relax? Are there parts of your body where you feel a lot of tension? For very tense areas, it helps to tense and release several times. Were you able to focus your attention on the relaxation? If other thoughts came into your mind, did you let them pass through? Did you feel more relaxed after the exercise? Did you feel any anxiety during the procedure? Repeated practice will let you go through the whole procedure without feeling anxious. Be aware that some anxiety may occur initially if you are sensitive to the sensations that are produced by relaxation, or to the sense of loss of control produced by the procedure. However, this reaction is, in fact, evidence that you should repeat the relaxation procedure.

Keep a record of each time you practice so you can observe over time how well you do with the relaxation and track any problems that you encounter. This record will provide a good source of feedback for you. On the Relaxation Record Form in your packet (see the example in Figure 5.2), keep a record of your levels of relaxation and concentration. As mentioned before, the exercise should be practiced twice a day for the next week.

If, at the end of 7 days, you are able to complete the 16-muscle-group procedure and feel relaxed as a result of the exercise (at least 4 on the 8–point scale of relaxation), you can move on to the 8-muscle-group procedure. On the other hand, if you are still experiencing difficulty relaxing, continue with the full 16-muscle-group procedure for an additional week. The 8-muscle-group procedure is the same as the 16-muscle-group procedures except that some muscle groups are excluded because of generalization. That is, by relaxing major areas of your body, other areas will also become relaxed. The muscle groups that we suggest for the 8-muscle-procedure are the arm as one unit (upper and lower), the leg as one unit (upper and lower), the stomach, the chest, the shoulders, the neck, the eyes, and

Relaxation Record

If doing breathing retraining ONLY, see other side.

See Figure 5.2 in your workbook.

0	1	2	3	4	5	6	7	8
None		**Mild**		**Moderate**		**Strong**		**Extreme**

For each practice, rate your relaxation and concentration according to the scale above.

Date	Practice	Relaxation at the end of the exercise	Concentration during the exercise
3/01	1	2	2
3/01	2	2	2
3/02	1	2	2
3/02	2	2	3
3/03	1	3	3
3/03	2	4	3
3/04	1	4	4
3/04	2	4	5
3/05	1	5	6
3/05	2	6	6
3/06	1	5	4
3/06	2	4	5
3/07	1	5	5
3/07	2	6	6

Copyright © 1994 Graywind Publications, Inc.   Mastery of Your Anxiety and Panic

Figure 5.2. Example of Relaxation Record Form

the forehead. However, if you find that there is one part of your body that becomes very tense, such as your jaw, then you might continue to include it in the procedure.

To relax the arms as one unit, simply tense the lower arm and the upper arms at the same time. Similarly relax the legs as one unit. Use the same procedure, focusing your attention on the tension feelings and the relaxation feelings, progressing from one muscle group to the next. At the end, count from 1 to 5 to become more relaxed, and then gradually come out of the relaxation while counting backward from 5 to 1. Practice the 8-muscle-procedure twice a day for 7 days and keep a record of your practices on the Relaxation Record Form. Monitoring will provide feedback on your progress. An outline of the relaxation procedure is provided below.

Outline for Relaxation Training

Step Description

1. Quiet location, comfortable chair or bed
2. Loosen tight clothing.
3. Tense for 10 seconds and relax for 20 seconds the following major muscle groups:

Step	Muscle group
1, 2	lower arms
3, 4	upper arms
5, 6	lower legs
7, 8	upper legs
9	abdomen
10	chest
11	shoulders
12	neck
13	mouth, throat, and jaw
14	eyes
15	lower forehead
16	upper forehead

4. Focus attention on sensations of tension and relaxation.
5. Count from one to five to deepen relaxation, breathe slowly for 2 minutes, and count from five to one to become more alert.
6. Practice two times per day for 7 days.
7. Monitor your practice.

8. Proceed to 8-muscle-group relaxation when able to relax using 16-muscle-group procedure.

1	upper and lower arms
2	upper and lower legs
3	abdomen
4	chest
5	shoulders
6	neck
7	eyes
8	forehead

Exercises

Breathing Control: Practice the breathing retraining exercise twice a day 10 minutes each time for 7 days. Keep a record of your practices on the Breathing Retraining Record Form. Continue to monitor your panics and anxiety using the methods described previously.

Relaxation Training: Practice the relaxation exercise twice a day for 7 days, proceeding from 16 muscle groups to 8 muscle groups when you feel comfortable and relaxed using the 16 muscle groups. Monitor your practice on the Relaxation Record Form. Continue to monitor your anxiety and panic using the methods described earlier.

Self-Assessment

Answer by circling **T** (True) or **F** (False). Answers are provided in Appendix A.

1. Overbreathing

   a. Overbreathing means breathing too much and too deeply for the body's needs at a particular point in time.   T   F

   b. Continuous overbreathing is potentially dangerous.   T   F

   c. When practicing breathing retraining exercises, you should focus on completely unrelated material.   T   F

   d. Speeding up of the breathing rate during the exercise is an indication to stop using breathing exercises.   T   F

    e. The goals of breathing retraining are to reduce the symptoms that may begin the panic reaction and to reduce overbreathing that may occur during panic and during general anxiety. **T F**

2. Muscular Tension

    a. Being physically tense all of the time means that you will never be able to relax. **T F**

    b. A lot of muscle tension feeds into cycles of anxious anticipation and fear. **T F**

    c. Symptoms such as fatigue, muscle aches and pains and weakness are often related to a high level of muscle tension. **T F**

    d. When doing relaxation exercises, one should try to attain complete relaxation in one initial step. **T F**

    e. The goals of relaxation training are to reduce symptoms that may begin the panic reaction and to reduce tension that occurs during panic and general anxiety. **T F**

3. Overbreathing is not a factor for most people who have panic attacks. **T F**

4. Feeling frightened while learning muscle relaxation is an indication that muscle relaxation will not be helpful to you and should be discontinued. **T F**

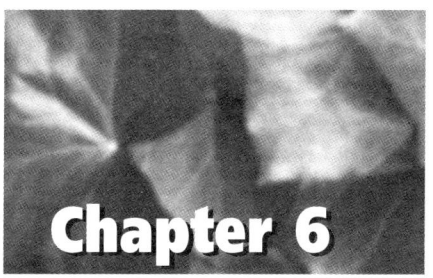

Chapter 6

Development of Control of Physical Responses

Review

Review your Daily Mood Record and Panic Attack Record from the last week and add the average anxiety and number of panics to your Progress Record Form. Did you notice any other patterns during the week? Were you able to analyze processes during times of fear? That is, did you look for cues to your panic and did you examine interactions among things you might have said to yourself and different feelings and sensations that you experienced? Now review your monitoring of practices for the breathing retraining and the relaxation. If you are working with the breathing retraining, continue with the next part of this chapter. If you are working with relaxation, skip to that section of this chapter.

Breathing Control

Did you feel as if you were getting enough air into the diaphragm? Remember, if you feel that you are not getting enough air, push the stomach out before inhaling. Are you having symptoms of anxiety when you practice? These symptoms are probably due to breathing a little fast or becoming sensitive to breathing patterns when you think about them. Keep practicing, and the anxiety will diminish. Are you having trouble concentrating on the counting? Practice will help your concentration, but if you continue to have difficulty concentrating, it may be helpful to make a tape for yourself on which you record counting at an appropriate rate. Examine your ratings on the Breathing Retraining Record for the week. Did the ease with which you could breathe "properly" improve? If not, think about some of the reasons suggested earlier and try to make changes based on these. Keep practicing because the techniques will become easier.

In the previous chapter, the aim was for you to match your counting with your breathing; that is, to count when inhaling and to think *relax* when exhaling.

From now on, in order to begin to slow the breathing rate, begin to match your breathing to your counting. That is, count the number and then inhale, think the word *relax* and then exhale. Gradually begin to slow your counting day by day until you can breathe at a rate of about 10 breaths per minute. This rate translates to about 3 seconds in and 3 seconds out. Continue to practice with one hand on your stomach and one hand on your chest in order to ensure that you are breathing from the diaphragm. Try this procedure now: *One*, breathe in; *relax*, breathe out; *two*, breathe in; *relax*, breathe out, and so on. Sometimes it is helpful to pause between each step, that is, before exhaling and before inhaling. You can experiment with this. The main points are to slow your breathing while maintaining a smooth and fluid cycle and to use the diaphragm more than the chest.

Continue to practice this procedure at least twice a day, monitoring your breathing and concentration with each practice and using the Breathing Retraining Record Form. Practice for the next 7 days, gradually slowing the rate of breathing to 10 breaths per minute.

Muscle Relaxation

Examine your Relaxation Record for the week. Did your levels of relaxation and concentration increase the more you practiced the exercises? Did you have any problems concentrating? If that was the case, remind yourself to bring your attention back each time you notice your thoughts wandering. Were you able to feel relaxation in different parts of your body? If you have certain muscle groups that are difficult to relax, try to practice tensing and releasing them several times. Did you feel too much pressure to do the relaxation? Had you not devoted enough time for the relaxation? These practices must be given priority in order to benefit from them. The amount you get out of these programs is a function of how much effort you put in.

If you feel comfortable with the 8-muscle-group procedure and your rating of relaxation is at least 4, it is time to break the exercise down to 4-muscle-groups. If you are still having some problems becoming relaxed, continue with the 16- or 8-muscle-group procedure for another week. For the 4-muscle-group procedure, the muscles we suggest tensing and releasing include the stomach, the chest, the shoulders, and the face as one unit (tense and relax all of your face muscles at one time). Again, if there are different parts of your body that are very tense, you might continue to include the related muscle groups. Use the same procedure described earlier; practice twice a day for the next week. Continue to practice in a relaxing environment and to monitor your levels of concentration and relaxation with each practice using the Relaxation Record Form.

Exercise

Practice your breathing or relaxation exercises twice a day over the next 7 days, continuing to monitor your practices using the Breathing Retraining Form or Relaxation Record Form. Continue to use your Daily Mood Record and Panic Attack Record. Remember, there are enough forms in the packet for you to complete the program. Pay special attention to the role of breathing patterns and muscle tension in your fearful reactions and generalized anxiety.

Self-Assessment

Answer by circling **T** (True) or **F** (False). Answers are provided in Appendix A.

1. Skipping out on practices once in a while is okay. **T F**

2. Attention during the exercises is very important. **T F**

3. If the exercise has not become any easier by now, then it is never going to work. **T F**

4. The monitoring of relaxation or breathing is necessary because it allows evaluation of progress and an objective understanding of how the techniques are being applied and their effectiveness. It is one part of learning control. **T F**

Chapter 7

Refinement of Physical Response Control Techniques and an Introduction to Self-Statement Analysis

Review

Review your Daily Mood Record and Panic Attack Record for the past week. Add your data to your Progress Record Form. Spend a few minutes thinking about patterns that emerged or responses that were different. Can you think of each episode of panic and anxiety in an objective way by understanding the sequence of events that preceded, occurred during, and followed the episode? Did you notice a spiral effect due to the interaction among different aspects of your thoughts, feelings, and behaviors?

Breathing Control

Now that you are able to breathe at a slower rate, it is time to begin practicing in different places. Do it when you are at work, watching television, or out socially. Do as many "minipractices" as you can during the day. In addition, begin to use the exercise when you become aware of feeling out of breath or anxious. As you feel the symptoms building, begin to concentrate on slow, smooth diaphragmatic breathing. Count on your inhalations and think the word *relax* on the exhalations. Continue by counting from one to ten and back down to one, slowing the breathing rate to about 3 seconds on the inhalation and 3 seconds on the exhalation. It is okay if the technique does not work at first. Just continue to practice the exercise, and, after each time you have used the technique, evaluate how well it worked and what, if anything, you could have done differently. Do not give up if it does not work right away because learning is almost always gradual. With practice you will learn to use breathing control as needed.

Also, remember that even if you do not control the symptoms of breathlessness, you are not in danger. This point is very important. To feel you must slow your breathing to prevent yourself from losing control or from having a heart attack adds anxiety to the breathing-control exercise. Remember, hyperventilation is not dangerous.

Relaxation Training

Now that you have been able to relax using 4 muscle groups, it is time for recall and cue-controlled relaxation. Instead of tensing up the muscles first, now try to relax each of the four major muscle groups by remembering the feelings of relaxation that you experienced during the past exercises. Focus on a muscle group and think about relaxing. Think about the sensations of relaxation such as heaviness, warmth, or floating. Progressively focus on each part of your body (for 20 seconds each time) and then count from one to five to achieve a deeper state of relaxation. Focus on slow, relaxing breathing for 1–2 minutes. Then count back from five to one. Gradually become more alert as you count back to one. This procedure may take more practice than the other exercises, because it requires intense concentration. As you recall the feeling of relaxation, describe as clearly as you can in your own mind these feelings in your body. For example, relaxing the muscles in your neck might be described as a heavy, drooping sensation. Or, it might seem as if you are cutting a tight cord that is holding your head and neck in a rigid position. Also, physically let go of the tension by movements such as drooping your shoulders down or letting your stomach relax outward. As you focus on becoming relaxed, continue to think to yourself the word *relax*. Repeat *relax* over and over again so that it becomes associated with the relaxed feelings. Later, you will learn to use that word as a signal for relaxation in the same way that sensations have become a signal for you to feel fearful.

Practice the recall procedure twice a day for the next 7 days or until you are able to relax by recall easily, that is, until you can achieve a relaxation rating of at least 4. Once you are able to do that, continue on to the next step.

The next step is called *cue relaxation*. This step relies on the meaning of the word *relax*. Think of the word *relax* and, as you think of that word, review your body and let go of all of the tension. Try it now. Again, this procedure might take more practice because of the concentration required. Try to practice it as often as you can, at any time that you have a few seconds to relax.

In addition, start to use cue relaxation in different places, such as waiting at a stoplight or walking down the street, so that it becomes a skill that you can apply when needed.

Also, apply cue relaxation when you notice physical tension in your body, feel anxious or panicky, or both. Use it as a control technique to gain mastery over your emotions. One important reason that the relaxation method works is that relaxing interferes with the tendency to escape or run. Staying put and relaxing is the opposite of escaping and fleeing. Relaxing when you feel agitation building becomes a competing response. Do not be frustrated if it does not work at first. Relaxation is a skill that requires practice.

Beginning of Self-Statement Analysis

We discussed in earlier chapters the importance of misinterpretations. A great deal of information was provided so you could develop a new understanding of panic and anxiety. Now, you will learn to use more direct techniques to change the statements you say to yourself. It is possible that the information in the earlier chapters has changed your overall perspective. You might still remain concerned about the possibilities of dying, going crazy, losing control, or being embarrassed during panic. For example, you might think, "When I am calm and relaxed, I realize that there is no chance that I will collapse the next time I panic, but when I am in the middle of a panic attack, I am almost convinced that I am about to collapse." The fact that negative thoughts become stronger or more believable in the midst of intense anxiety is called mood–thought congruency. That is, certain thoughts are more likely to occur during certain emotions. It is easier to remember sad events when we are depressed than when we are happy. Similarly, thoughts of harm and danger are more likely to occur at times of anxiety than at relaxed times. The important point is that having more thoughts about danger, for example, "I am having a heart attack," does not mean that it is more likely to occur. That is, thinking about having a heart attack does not make a heart attack more likely. In other words, anxiety brings more negative thoughts to mind, but neither the anxiety nor the thoughts make the likelihood of actual danger any greater than if you were relaxed.

Although these negative thoughts are not accurate, they create anxiety. Remember the model of anticipatory anxiety and fear of fear described in the earlier chapters. The thoughts take part in panic attacks in two ways. First, negative thoughts about the future (e.g., "What if I panic when I am giving my speech tomorrow?") can increase anxious arousal. This arousal can lead to physical sensations that are triggers for panic. Second, after the triggering sensation is noticed, misinterpretations (e.g., "I am going to faint") contribute to the cycle of fear of fear.

Therefore, it is important to modify anxious thinking. Modifying what you tell yourself, in effect, changes the structure of panic. By changing your self-statements, you will eliminate a big part of the panic reaction and, therefore, reduce the frequency of panic attacks.

You might also be saying, "I don't tell myself anything when I panic, it just comes out of the blue." As mentioned earlier, there is a dimension of conscious awareness of thought processes. That is, sometimes you may be strongly aware of thinking very frightening things, and, at other times, your thoughts may be automatic so that you are not aware of their influence. Two experts on this topic, Aaron T. Beck and Gary Emery (1985), have termed this *automaticity* and *discreteness in cognitions*. The term *automatic* means that the thoughts occur rapidly and may be outside of direct awareness. The term *discrete* refers to the fact that these thoughts are very specific and may vary across situations. The focus of your worry may differ from one situation to another; you may be concerned mostly about embarrassment in one situation and mostly about being without help in another situation.

The implication is that sometimes you have to search very hard for the particular thoughts that are present, and it is important to pursue the thoughts until you identify a specific prediction. Identifying the thought as "I felt terrible" is too global and may serve to increase your anxiety by being so nondirective. Further analysis is necessary. What do you picture happening? What do you think could happen as a result of feeling terrible?

Review each episode of anxiety and panic that you have self-monitored over the last few weeks. What were the major thoughts before, during, and after the episodes? Are your descriptions general, such as "I felt horrible" or "I felt anxious"? If so, try to remember the event as it occurred and try to think of what you said to yourself at that time. Why was it so terrible? What did you think could happen? What do you think would happen if you panicked then? What would it mean if you felt like you were going to lose control? Here is an example of identifying negative thoughts.

> **I was afraid that if I went into the store I would feel very anxious, start to look for a way out, and then panic and not know how to get out. I would feel like I would have to get out because if I stayed in that store and panicked, I could really lose control. Losing control would mean that I would become overwhelmed by the feeling of anxiety and I couldn't stand it. Being overwhelmed means that the feelings could get really intense, and I would be afraid that I would explode or go crazy because the feelings are so intense. I have an image of people gathering around me, trying to restrain me, and then being taken away by the police.**

Once you are able to be this specific as to what you are thinking, the thought is much more open to challenge. Stopping at the point of "I am afraid" does not allow for changing the way you think. Therefore, it is important to pursue the thoughts as far as you can by continuing to question them. If you do not question them, you cannot reduce your anxiety and panic.

Remember Jill, whom we introduced in earlier chapters. When she first attended our clinic, Jill was very sensitive to changes in her heart rate. Her first statements were "It's just a horrible feeling—and I can get so afraid that I become totally out of control." In this statement, Jill used two global descriptions—that the feeling is horrible and that she totally loses control. Here is how the therapist helped Jill become aware of the bases for her descriptions.

T: What do you mean when you say that the feeling of a racing heart is horrible? What is horrible about it?

J: Well, it makes me feel very scared.

T: What are you scared of?

J: It makes me worry about something going wrong—physically.

T: What do you think could happen?

J: Maybe, no, I definitely feel that my heart will just keep going faster and faster and eventually it will stop.

T: And then what?

J: Well, then I'll die.

T: So, actually your statement that the feeling of a racing heart is horrible is based on a series of images leading up to your death. Those are really negative. It makes sense that you would be feeling so anxious, given what it is that you think could happen. What about your fears of totally losing control? What do you mean by that?

J: That's hard to describe. I guess I don't really know what it means. I just feel out of control.

T: Well, what do you think could happen if you were totally out of control?

J: That I couldn't stop the way I was feeling.

T: And what would happen if you couldn't stop the feeling?

J: Well, the feeling would get so intense that I wouldn't be able to function any more. I'd just be a wreck.

T: And then what?

J: Well, that would be the end of my life. I'd spend the rest of my life doing nothing.

T: So, again, the statement of losing control is based on some quite specific predictions you are making.

As you can see, when pursued, the nature of Jill's thoughts became clearer. From that point on, it was easier to dispel her fears about losing control and heart disease.

Identifying Probability Overestimation

There are two general types of "errors" in thoughts that are important to anxiety and panic. The first one is called *probability overestimation*. Can you think of any times when you caught yourself jumping to a negative conclusion only later to find out that you were wrong? Think of examples that are relevant to both general anxiety and to panic. A typical example of overestimation in general anxiety is "Nothing will get done on time." A typical panic example is "I will faint." Review the list of negative thoughts that you identified for each panic attack over the last few weeks. Now ask yourself if any of the events you feared would happen actually occurred. What does the result tell you?

You might say, "Yes, I know those things are not going to happen but I still get frightened by the possibility." Why these thought errors occur despite repeated proof to the contrary? Why does a person continue to be afraid of going crazy or continue to be afraid of passing out, despite the fact that panic has occurred hundreds of times without the person's ever going crazy or passing out?

There are several reasons that negative thoughts persist despite lack of evidence:

- One reason is believing that the event could still happen; this thought reflects a dismissal of all previous experiences that have shown that panic attacks are survivable and reflects judgments based on emotional reasoning rather than on facts. This thinking is similar to the illogical belief that because none of your air flights have crashed to date, then a crash is even more likely on the next flight, as though the probabilities accumulate over time. Although it is true that probabilities do eventually accumulate, this is relevant only for events that are likely in the first place. For a plane crash, which has a probability of 1 in 10 million, the likelihood of a crash does not significantly increase whether you fly 10 times or 500 times. A similar logic applies to the things that you think could happen if you panicked.

- Another reason is believing after the panic attack is over that "I was lucky that time" instead of realizing the error of the original prediction. An example is saying, "If I had not gone to the emergency room, I don't know what would have happened." Real evidence is ignored or distorted to fit into the bias of interpreting that there was danger. Many times we have heard clients say such things as "It would have been terrible if I hadn't found my husband" or "I know I was really on the edge of totally losing it" or "I don't know how I survived it, I'm sure I wouldn't be able to go through another one like that." All

"The fuel light's on, Frank! We're all going to die! ... Wait, wait ... Oh, my mistake – that's the intercom light."

of these statements are based on biased interpretations of what happened, instead of on the realization that panic was survived because there was no real danger.

- Third, people sometimes misconstrue past events as a sign of the very thing they are afraid of happening. We referred to this notion before when discussing the concept of loss of control. Sometimes the feeling of panic and the urge to escape are seen as signs of loss of control when, in fact, panic is better viewed as a state of overcontrol. That is, behavior becomes goal-directed during panic to escape the "danger." If you believe that you are about to stop breathing, then it makes sense to run outside into fresh air. If you believe that you are about to have a stroke, then it makes sense to go to a hospital. However, if you view that behavior as being out of control, then it also makes sense that you would continue to fear losing control in the future, because in your mind the evidence suggests that loss of control is a real possibility.

The misbelief that the stronger the anxiety or the sensations of arousal are, the more likely the perceived danger will happen. For example, "I know I haven't lost all touch with reality yet, but what if the feelings get worse than ever before . . . then I really could flip out." This thinking reflects the misbelief that intensity of sensations increases risk, when this is not the case at all.

Finally, negative overestimations continue because of the associations that have built up over time. It is likely that negative thoughts will come into your mind when you are anxious despite your logical understanding at other times that they are not accurate. However, that does not mean that they should not be analyzed for their accuracy. Just because a thought comes into your mind does not mean that it is accurate: Worrying about losing control does not mean you will lose control and worrying about dying does not mean you will die. Instead of treating those thoughts as reasons to become more frightened, evaluate them objectively.

Some of these types of reasoning are illustrated in the interaction between one of our clients, Jane, and her therapist:

J: Several times I thought I was really going to lose it this time . . . that I would flip out and never return to reality. It never actually happened, but it could still happen.

T: Why do you think it could still happen?

J: Part of me feels like I've always managed to escape it just in time, by either removing myself from the situation, or by having my husband help me, or by holding on long enough for the feelings to pass. But what if next time I can't hold on?

T: Given our discussion earlier about the nature of anxious thinking, can you classify any of your ideas as overestimations?

J: I suppose you're saying that in reality I can always hold on or that I can always escape in time.

T: More that you feel a need to hold on and the need to escape because you are overestimating the likelihood of flipping out and never returning to reality.

J: But it really feels like I will.

T: The confusion between what you think will happen and what actually happens is the very problem that we are addressing in this phase of the treatment.

Examine some of your negative panic predictions and determine whether they are overestimations. Use predictions from past and future events. For past events, did you tell yourself that unless you had called someone or gotten out of the situation when you panicked, you would not have survived? If so, then you are most likely overestimating the danger. For future events, are you predicting that the next time you panic you could really lose control? In Jane's case, as soon as she became aware that the reason she was afraid of losing control was because she predicted that the panic would never stop, she realized that her prediction was inaccurate, because, indeed, her panic attacks, like those of everyone else, were very brief.

You can conduct the same kind of analysis with general anxiety. For example, an overestimation of a past event might be "my boss was angry with me last week when he did not smile during our conversation." An example of a future overestimation might be "I got through it this time, but next time I have people over for dinner, I'm sure that everything will result in a failure."

Challenging Probability Overestimation

The basis for challenging these overestimations is to question the evidence for your judgments. Remember to treat thoughts as hypotheses or guesses rather than as facts. Before you make a judgment, you should examine the evidence for it. Your interpretation is one of many possible interpretations. Your interpretation may be very different from that of someone else. So, it is important to explore alternatives. This is especially important because when an individual is anxious, he or she tends to be biased in his or her interpretations. Think of your anxiety on a spectrum with neutral or no anxiety at the midpoint, extreme anxiety at one end, and extreme calmness at the other. If you view an impending situation with dread because you think something bad might happen, your emotion is going to be charged toward the anxiety end. On the other hand, if you view the same situation with a carefree attitude, your emotion will be charged toward the calmness end. In other words, you can create an emotional state in either direction. Obviously, the goal is not to remove anxiety about real threats but to lessen the anxious bias when there is no real threat.

To evaluate the evidence, ask yourself what the real odds of an event's happening are. Has this ever happened before? What is the evidence that it will or will not happen? This analysis means you must look at all of the facts before you predict how likely something is. For example, you may assume that you are going to fail a test and ignore the fact that you have prepared carefully. A friend may be acting coldly, and you may think she or he is displeased with you, overlooking that your friend may be angry with someone else or has had a bad day. In terms of panic, you may assume that the tingling in your left arm is a sign of a heart attack, overlooking the fact that you are in good health and that you have experienced the tingling many times before without having a heart attack. Certainly, Jane was overlooking the fact that none of her panic attacks had ever continued forever. It is possible that you are making negative predictions on the basis of a limited set of past examples. For example, you may predict that you will fail an exam or become anxious because you have done poorly on similar exams or have become anxious in similar situations before. However, you may be overlooking many instances in which you have done well on such exams or were not anxious in those situations. You may, in fact, be confusing low probabilities with high probabilities. You may also act or feel as if negative outcomes are certainties rather than possibilities. Such unrealistic statements are "I know I am going to panic the next time I go into the mall" and "I know I am going to have an accident at some time in the near future."

In challenging overestimations, you will find it helpful to consider the type of logic that you use to reach the conclusion that something bad might happen. This point is reflected in the following interchange between Jane and her therapist:

T: One of the specific self-statements you have identified is that you will flip out and never return to reality. What specifically leads you to think that this is likely to happen?

J: Well, I guess it really feels like that.

T: Be more specific if you can. What feelings?

J: Well, I feel spacy and unreal, like things around me are different and that I'm not connected.

T: And why do you think those feelings mean that you have lost touch with reality?

J: I don't know. It feels as if I have.

T: Well, do you respond if someone asks you a question at those times?

J: Well, I respond to you even though I feel that way sometimes in here.

T: Okay, and can you walk or write or drive when you feel that way?

J: Yes, but it feels different.

T: Okay, so you feel different, and yet you perform those functions despite feeling detached. So, what does that tell you?

J: Well, maybe I haven't lost complete touch with reality, but what if I do?

T: How many times have you felt detached?

J: Hundreds of times.

T: And how many times have you lost touch with reality permanently?

J: Never . . . but what if the feelings don't go away, maybe I'll lose it then.

T: So, what else tells you that this is a possibility?

J: Well, what about my second cousin. He lost it when he was about 25, and now he's just a mess. He can hardly do anything on his own, and he is constantly in and out of psychiatric wards. They have him on a bunch of heavy-duty drugs. I'll never forget the time I saw him totally out of it at his home—He was talking to himself in gibberish. They said he was psychotic.

T: Do you think you'll be like your cousin because he is suffering a condition that you fear? What about if another cousin had back problems—Would you become afraid of suffering back problems?

J: I suppose not, because having back problems doesn't scare me.

T: So, let's consider all of the evidence and some alternatives. You have felt unreal hundreds of times, and you've never lost touch with reality because you've continued to function in the midst of those feelings, and they have never

>   lasted forever. You are afraid of becoming like your cousin even though after further discussion we can see that there is little reason to assume that what he is experiencing is anything like what you are going through. Also, keep in mind our previous discussion of where feelings of unreality can come from, that is, from anxious arousal and overbreathing. So, what is the realistic probability that you will lose touch with reality permanently? Use a scale from 0 to 100 points, where 0 is *no chance at all* and 100 is *definitely will happen.*
>
> **J:** Well, maybe it is lower than I thought. Maybe 20%.
>
> **T:** So, that would mean that you have actually lost touch with reality in a permanent way once every five times you have felt unreal?
>
> **J:** When it's put like that, I guess not. Maybe it's a very small possibility.
>
> **T:** Yes, so what is an alternative explanation?
>
> **J:** Perhaps the feelings of unreality are caused by feeling anxious or overbreathing, and having those feelings does not mean that I am actually losing touch with reality and that I am not like my cousin at all.

Take your own examples of overestimations and examine the evidence for each. Just asking yourself for evidence means that you interrupt the emotional cycle and prevent yourself from being "carried along" or controlled by the fear. Become an objective observer. To help you do this, use the form entitled Modifying Self-Statements: 1. Overestimating, in your packet. If you prefer, you can make up your own page with examples of overestimations in the left column, evidence for each example in the middle column, and realistic probabilities in the right column. Remember to keep in mind typical errors in logic that could be driving your fears. These include assumptions that the more intense the anxiety and the sensations, the greater the risk, or that a little anxiety reflects complete loss of control, or that trying to escape a situation reflects loss of control. These errors in logic can be challenged. Also, remember to consider how you reached your conclusion, such as when Jane made a connection between herself and her cousin. The important thing for Jane to realize was that having a cousin with schizophrenia did not mean that she would have similar problems and that her feelings of unreality did not reflect a psychotic process.

Modifying Self-Statements
1. Overestimating

See Figure 7.1 in your workbook.

Write examples of your overestimations.
Then list alternative evidence.
Finally, rate the realistic probability of each feared event.

Overestimation errors	Alternative evidence	Realistic probability (0–100)
1. I could faint the next time I panic.	What are the real chances of fainting? What is the probability on a 0-100 point scale? Have I ever fainted before?	5%
2. I could have a car accident when I feel dizzy while driving.	What evidence do I have? How many times have I felt dizzy when driving and how many times have I had a car accident when feeling dizzy?	5%
3. If I'm left alone I'll really lose it and go crazy.	What has happened in the past when I've been alone? Or, have I ever tested out my reaction to see what would happen if I was alone? I might feel anxious, but what evidence do I have that I would go crazy?	2%
4. The pains in my chest must mean that I'm having a heart attack.	What is the evidence against this possibility? What were the results from my last medical check-up? How many times have I felt the pain before? Have I ever had a heart attack?	5%

Copyright © 1994 Graywind Publications, Inc.   Mastery of Your Anxiety and Panic

Figure 7.1. Example of Modifying Self-Statement—Overestimations Form

It is helpful to rate the actual probability of the feared event (as was shown in the previous example) after you have examined all of the evidence and challenged all of the misassumptions. Rate the probability on a 100-point scale, where 0 means *it will never happen*, and 100 means *it will definitely happen*. In this way, you are building a new structure of thoughts that more accurately represents reality.

A list of examples of how to identify and challenge thoughts is provided in Figure 7.1.

Exercise

In addition to continuing with breathing control or relaxation throughout the day (or both), pay special attention to errors of overestimation in your thoughts. (You no longer need to monitor your practice of the breathing or relaxation exercise.) If episodes of panic or anxiety have not occurred recently, think about past episodes and identify the thoughts you had and how they could be subjected to a more evidence-based analysis. Continue to use your Daily Mood Record and Panic Attack Record.

Self-Assessment

Answer by circling **T** (True) or **F** (False). Answers are provided in Appendix A.

1. Thoughts have no impact on how one feels.   **T F**

2. Part of changing one's thoughts or self-statements involves being very specific in the description of thoughts.   **T F**

3. This kind of analysis doesn't work because what I am afraid of could still happen.   **T F**

4. Questioning what one thinks interrupts the emotional cycle and allows one to gain control.   **T F**

5. Although fearful negative thoughts are likely to be stronger or more believable during periods of intense anxiety or panic, this does not mean that they are any more likely to come true than when you are relaxed.   **T F**

6. It is possible for anxious thoughts to occur rapidly and out of your direct awareness, and this can contribute to the feeling that your panics occur for no reason or from "out of the blue."   **T F**

Chapter 8

Continuation of Self-Statement Analysis Manipulating Your Own Mind

Review

Review your Daily Mood Record and Panic Attack Record from the past week. Add your data to your Progress Record Form. Spend a few minutes thinking about patterns that have emerged or responses that differ from those of past weeks. Did you examine each panic and anxiety episode step-by-step? Did you begin by identifying the initial trigger for your anxiety or panic episode? Were you able to analyze the interaction among your physical sensations, behaviors, and thoughts? Did you notice the relationship between the interaction of your physical sensations, thoughts, and behaviors and the resulting consequence? Were you an objective observer of your own responses?

Breathing Retraining

Did you use breathing control at times when you felt out of breath or anxious? What was the effect? Did you try this strategy with a sense of desperation, to escape or prevent, at all costs, the symptoms of anxiety? If so, remember the purpose of this strategy. Breathing retraining is not designed to prevent a terrible event, that is, panic or suffocation, from happening. Rather, it is designed to target the physical component of anxiety. It is important that you use the strategy within that context. If you are using breathing retraining with desperation, you add fuel to the fire and thereby increase anxiety. By fighting, you are adding to the intensity. Remember, even if you never learn to slow your breathing, you will survive.

Were you able to pick up on early signals, or was it not until you found yourself gasping for breath that you tried the technique? If this was the case, try to become more aware of signs that should prompt you to exercise breathing control. Continue to apply the breathing strategy whenever you notice yourself becoming anxious or feeling short of breath, until the strategy becomes a natural response.

Relaxation Training

Were you able to apply relaxation, using the cue-controlled format, when tense, anxious or panicky? Were you able to discriminate levels of tension in your body and apply relaxation upon first noticing the tension? Did you wait until you became extremely tense and rigid before applying the strategy? If the latter was the case, try to become more aware of the earlier signs of tension that should prompt you to apply relaxation. However, this awareness should not be confused with an attempt to prevent anxiety or panic at all costs. Did you use relaxation as a method of escaping a catastrophe? Remember, relaxation is not intended as an escape or avoidance strategy, which is used in a desperation mode. Rather, it is intended to reduce symptoms that contribute to the anxiety and panic spiral. Continue to use the relaxation as a strategy over the following week at times when you notice feeling anxious, frightened, or tense.

Catastrophic Thinking

Did you pay attention to your thinking patterns over the past week and notice times when you were overestimating the likelihood of negative events? Did you challenge those errors by questioning the evidence? Do not be discouraged if such questioning seems artificial at first or does not immediately result in feeling less anxious. As with the other exercises, thinking exercises require practice, because you are learning to replace an old habit of responding with a new one.

The second type of "error" in the way that an individual processes information is when feeling anxious or frightened is called *catastrophic thinking*. In addition to being frightened of an event that is unlikely to happen, that is, overestimating, an individual might view an event as "dangerous," "insufferable," or "catastrophic" when actually it is not. Here are some typical catastrophic thoughts: "If other people noticed that I was feeling very anxious or panicking, it would be terrible and I could never face them again." "It would be disastrous if I fainted." "If everything is not perfect when my friends visit, I will be a failure." "It would be horrible if I felt anxious." When thinking like this, the individual responds with increased anxiety and fear, without ever stopping to examine the validity of the thoughts. If you stop to examine the situation realistically, it is usually not as awful as it seemed at first. For example, fainting from acute hyperventilation, although unlikely, is not such a terrible event. Fainting is actually a mechanism that helps to reestablish a balance in the body, and the worst that can happen is a brief feeling of disorientation after regaining consciousness. Similarly, if another person noticed that you felt anxious, the worst that might happen is that the person would feel sympathy for you. If someone does negatively judge you, the worst that can happen is that the person will not think of you in the way you would like.

"Maybe it's *not* me, y'know?... Maybe it's the *rest* of the ..herd that's gone insane."

Catastrophic thinking means "blowing things out of proportion." Decatastrophizing is putting things back into perspective, partly by realizing what you could do to cope in a negative situation. For example, if someone mentioned that you looked anxious, you might say, "Yes, I've had a really tough week and I'm really wired right now," or "Yes, this is one of those tough situations for me." Decatastrophizing also entails the realization that you can get through many difficult situations - that it is possible to "ride through" a panic attack or to survive being embarrassed. Therefore, you can see that challenging these thoughts does not mean just positive thinking.

Think about the worst things you envision happening when you are anxious or panicky. Review the episodes of anxiety and panic that you have recorded over the past 2 weeks and determine whether any of your thoughts were catastrophic. Think of times when you have said to yourself, "That would be terrible" or "I couldn't stand it" or, in reference to the future, "I couldn't stand to live through that again." Similarly, a thought such as "I am so frightened that I might slip back into the way I felt several months ago when I was panicking more frequently—I couldn't stand to go through that again" is very catastrophic. If that is what you say to yourself, it is only natural to be distressed. One of our clients was anxious because she believed that she would not be able to cope mentally or physically with any more panic attacks—that the *big* one was going to destroy her. Therefore, she was constantly anxious and on guard for the next attack. Instead of trying to understand what panic attacks really are and instead of realizing that she had coped with all of her previous attacks, she focused on not being able to survive.

Another common thought is "Anything could happen the next time I panic, and that is what frightens me. I don't know what it is but it is going to be something bad." Again, this kind of thought generates anxiety. On the other hand, if you examine the evidence and consider the worst that can happen, it is not as bad as you first think. Remember to pull apart the emotion and the thought. It may feel bad, but the main reason that it feels bad is the negative thinking. Once you learn to identify and modify that thinking, you will not feel so bad.

Examples of catastrophic thinking in relation to more general anxiety include "I felt as if I was on the verge of a nervous breakdown and could not cope with anything or anyone when I had to deal with all those pressures at work last summer" and "I'll drop out of school and be a failure for the rest of my life if I don't pass the exam." Can you classify any of your own self-statements into the category of catastrophic thinking?

To challenge these self-statements, critically evaluate the actual severity of feared events. This kind of analysis can be conducted with events that are likely to happen, for example, shaking when you feel anxious in a public situation, and events that are unlikely to happen, for example, fainting in the midst of a panic attack. If the worst that is considered likely to happen is death or loss of significant others or behaviors that go against religious beliefs, then decatastrophizing may not be as effective. Generally, analysis of probability is more appropriate for fears of death or loss. That is, how likely is it that you will die the next time you panic, and how likely is it that you will do something against your beliefs?

Ask yourself what the worst thing is that could happen the next time you panic or that could happen in any situation that worries you? What if you actually did faint when you panicked? What if you actually did look shaky? What if you actually did walk out of a room because you felt trapped? Your first reaction to these questions might be something like "that would be awful or terrible" or "I couldn't stand it." However, when you think critically about these assumptions, you will find that you have prematurely assumed them to be worse than they are. For example, what would happen if people really did think you looked foolish because you were shaky and sweaty? Does it really matter what these people think? If they are strangers, then why should it matter what they think? You are unlikely to ever see them again. If they are friends, then this incident is not going to change their opinion of you, so, again it does not matter. What if people did think poorly of you? Does that mean you will never enjoy life again? In other words, you can stand or tolerate or bear any misfortune that happens to you. It is only the belief that you cannot stand the misfortune that creates the anxiety. In its most extreme form, decatastrophizing means that anybody can stand anything until he or she dies, and then there is no reason to stand it anymore. Decatastrophizing can be summed up in one phrase—So what! So what if I faint? So what if I look foolish? Jill provides an example. In Chapter 3, we used her panic attacks to show the sequence of events that results in panic. In one of her examples, Jill described being afraid and embarrassed if she panicked in a restaurant. When asked to specify further what would make her feel embarrassed, she said she would appear so terrified that everyone would know how she felt and would, therefore, think that she was weird. In addition to helping Jill realize she was overestimating the probability of others' noticing her and thinking she was weird, the therapist helped Jill understand that she was catastrophizing what others might think. Furthermore, even if she was upset about others thinking she was weird, that would not last forever. Here is another example:

T: What is so bad about your heart racing and feeling dizzy?

J: It's such a horrible feeling, I hate it. I wish the symptoms would just go away.

T: But what makes it so bad?

J: Because I can't get rid of the symptoms.

T: And what if we were to make it a ruling that you would have a racing heart and dizziness for the rest of your life?

J: I couldn't stand it.

T: What would you do? Let's make it easier. Let's say that you developed a disease that meant that for the rest of your life you would have pain in your left wrist. Now, what would you do to cope with that?

J: Well, I guess that I would try to do the best that I could. Maybe I'd do some exercises to relieve the pain. I'd probably continue to do most things that I do now, but perhaps not as easily.

T: Okay, so you would cope. Now, how is that different from a racing heart and feeling dizzy?

J: I feel like I can't do anything when I feel those symptoms.

T: Are you overestimating? What can you not do?

J: You're right . . . it's probably that I just think I can't do things. I mean, even though I feel those symptoms, I still read, talk to people, and drive around. Maybe I could do other things that I've been avoiding because I didn't think I could manage, like playing sports again.

T: Good. Now, when you realize that a racing heart and dizziness are manageable, do you see how the feelings themselves are likely to diminish?

You may find as you begin to focus on these kinds of images and thoughts that your anxiety increases. The reason is that the thoughts are anxiety provoking. There may still be some disbelief on your part that needs to be challenged. In other words, you may still feel deep down that the probability is high that you will die. In addition, you might have tried to avoid thoughts in the past because they frighten you. However, you will find that the thoughts become less anxiety provoking as you face them. Only by facing them directly can you evaluate whether the consequences would indeed be as intolerable as you believe them to be and realize that the anxiety or the embarrassment that you consider to be unbearable is actually *time limited* and *manageable*.

One common thought is that the anxiety and panic will continue forever. This thought reflects both overestimating and catastrophizing. The concept of "continuing forever" implies an inability to cope and a sense of vulnerability. A sense of vulnerability is usually based on overestimating and catastrophic thinking—an important point to remember. Apply this kind of evaluation to the thoughts you have had over the past couple of weeks. Use the Modifying Self-Statements II—Catastrophizing Form to list your major catastrophic thoughts and challenges. A list of examples is provided in Figure 8.1.

It is now up to you to use these strategies when you feel anxious or panicky. It would help to review periodically the previous two chapters because sometimes these types of thoughts seem stronger when you are in the midst of anxiety. To help control bias in your thinking, use the Self-Statement Rating Form in your packet. Identify the major concern when you are panicky and the major concern when you are generally anxious. Once a week, record your estimates of the probability that the event will happen when you panic and of how well you could cope if the event did happen. Do the same for your general anxiety concerns. Rate the probability and coping ability on a 100-point scale, where 0 means *no chance of*

Modifying Self-Statements
2. Catastrophizing

See Figure 8.1 in your workbook.

List your major catastrophic thoughts
and ways to challenge each one.

Catastrophizing (What if . . .)	Decatastrophizing (So what!)
1. What if I did faint in front of a lot of people? That would be terrible.	If I fainted there would be a reason and my body would be reestablishing a balance. The people around me would not know what was going on. They would try to help. What if they did think I fainted because I was nervous? Does it matter what they think? So what?
2. What if I was shaking terribly when talking to other people? What if they thought I was crazy?	Do I know these people? If they are strangers, does it matter what they think? If they are friends, no matter what they think at that time we will still be friends. Anyway, I can still live through the embarrassment.
3. What if I'm trapped in the elevator for an hour and panic the whole time? I couldn't cope.	Yes, I might feel anxious for the whole time I'm in there, but what else can happen? So what if I'm anxious?
4. My whole life is terrible; I can't go on. One day I'll just collapse and that will be the end.	Let's say I did reach a point of physical and mental exhaustion and I "collapsed"; meaning, I would become withdrawn and immobile. After some time of recovery I would be back up again. I would survive.

Copyright © 1994 Graywind Publications, Inc.   Mastery of Your Anxiety and Panic

Figure 8.1. Example of Modifying Self-Statements II—Catastrophizing Form

the event happening and no ability to cope, and 100 means *definitely will occur and complete ability to cope*. Rate these on the basis of your objective understanding, not in terms of how you feel. Over time you should see a decrease in probabilities and an increase in your estimates of coping ability. Both reflect the development of control over your emotions. For Jill, her most disturbing panic thought was that she would be the focus of attention and others would think she was crazy. At first she rated the probability to be quite high and her ability to cope very low (see Figure 8.2). Over time, however, you can see the changes. In terms of general anxiety she was concerned about the health of her child. With time, she realized that even if he did become ill, she would be able to cope. Rate your estimates now on the first-week line.

Exercise

Over the next week, continue to apply breathing control or relaxation when you notice physical symptoms or anxiety. Also, continue to use your Daily Mood Record and Panic Attack Record. In addition, be aware of any errors in your thinking (overestimation or catastrophizing) and challenge them. Specifically, at the end of each day, review your Panic Attack and Daily Mood Records. For each panic and anxiety episode, go through the following steps.

1. Identify thoughts or self-statements before and after the episode.

2. Determine whether these thoughts were overestimations or catastrophic thinking or both.

3. Examine the evidence and ask yourself "So what?"

You can use the Modifying Self-Statements I and II for each episode of anxiety and panic.

It is extremely important that you review your high anxiety and panic in this way. By doing so, you will learn to apply these more helpful styles of thinking when you do feel anxious or fearful. Do not be disheartened if, when you are anxious, it is more difficult to challenge these self-statements. Keep working at it, and it will become easier.

Self-Statement Rating Form

See Figure 8.2 in your workbook.

```
0   10   20   30   40   50   60   70   80   90   100
```
No probability/   **Definitely will occur/**
No ability to cope   **Complete ability to cope**

Write your major concern when you are panicky and your major concern when you are anxious. Each week for each event, rate what you think is the probability it will occur and your ability to cope with the event if it does occur. Use the scale above for your ratings.

	Panic/Fear		Anxiety	
	Event: *Others will think I'm crazy*		Event: *My son will get sick*	
Week	Probability it will occur	How well I can cope if it does occur	Probability it will occur	How well I can cope if it does occur
1st	80	10	75	20
2nd	70	10	50	30
3rd	60	40	50	40
4th	40	60	50	45
5th	30	70	50	55
6th	10	75	50	80

Copyright © 1994 Graywind Publications, Inc.   Mastery of Your Anxiety and Panic

Figure 8.2.   **Example of Self-Statement Rating Form**

Self-Assessment

Answer by circling **T** (True) or **F** (False). Answers are provided in Appendix A.

1. The fact that I have thoughts about being overwhelmed or collapsing means that these things are actually going to happen. **T F**

2. No one else has these kinds of thoughts. I must be really crazy. **T F**

3. Even if it is difficult to think more rationally when I am feeling very anxious or panicky, I should continue to try to understand what I am saying to myself, how that is adding to the fear, and how to change those statements. **T F**

4. Forcing myself to think about the worst that could happen will make me anxious initially, but the more I think about it in an objective way, the less anxious I will feel. **T F**

5. Breathing control is necessary to learn in order to prevent the occurrence of a terrible event such as panic or suffocation. **T F**

6. Identifying and altering one's automatic and incorrect thinking patterns, unlike learning breathing control or relaxation, does not require much practice because once you learn the general concept, then challenging one's beliefs is easy to do. **T F**

7. A panic attack will not continue forever. It is time-limited and manageable. If you do nothing, it will pass. **T F**

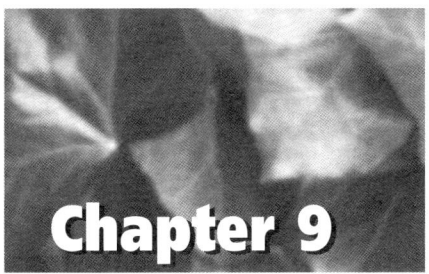

Chapter 9

The Unexpected Becomes Predictable

Review

Review your Daily Mood Record and Panic Attack Record for the past week. Add your data to your Progress Record Form. Spend a few minutes thinking about patterns that emerged or responses that were different. Can you think of each episode of panic and anxiety in an objective way by understanding the sequence of events that preceded, occurred during, and followed the episode? On your Self-Statement Rating Form, and record your probability and coping judgments. Have they changed from last week? If not, try to determine why. Are you ignoring evidence or are you catastrophizing?

Breathing Control and Relaxation Training

Were you able to use breathing-control and relaxation strategies when you felt symptoms or were anxious? Did you use them as a response strategy rather than as a desperate attempt to escape the feelings? Were you able to apply them when you first noticed the symptoms instead of waiting until the symptoms were very intense? Continue to use these techniques—make them a natural part of your behavior.

Self-Statements

At times, when you have felt anxious or panicky, have you been able to identify the specific thoughts going through your mind? Have you labeled them as overestimations or as catastrophic thinking or as both? Were you able to challenge self-statements? Were you able to say "So what"? It might feel artificial and forced at first to always examine and challenge your thoughts. However, as you practice, this style of thinking will become more natural. Although you might tell yourself now that the likelihood of a heart attack is slim, you might feel it is still possible. Keep working with it, and your belief will change.

It is also important to avoid the trap of using self-statement modification to "get rid of the physical sensations immediately." Remember, the goal of self-statement modification is to correct the incorrect thinking that contributes to fear and anxiety. In turn, reduction in fear and anxiety will lessen the physical sensations. However, the reduction in sensations does not always occur right away. For example, perhaps you have been out walking and you start to feel dizzy and scared. You identify the negative thought as "This dizziness makes me feel as if I am about to faint." You challenge the negative thought with "I have felt dizzy many times before and I have never fainted, so it is very unlikely that I will faint. The dizziness is just an uncomfortable sensation probably due to a change in my breathing or my anxiety level." Then, you notice that you are still feeling dizzy. This does not mean that your self-statement challenge was incorrect. Rather, it means that the dizziness will take a while to dissipate. Realizing that you are not in danger will certainly reduce the fearfulness, though, and increase the rate at which the dizziness subsides in contrast to what would happen if you told yourself you were indeed about to faint.

Finally, remember that you are learning a new skill. Therefore, it takes time for constructive thoughts to become more powerful than the old ways of thinking. For this reason, it is not unusual for negative thoughts to continue to reappear after they have been challenged with more realistic thoughts. So, at first you should expect to work through a series of challenges for the same negative thought. Just repeat the process over and over again.

Prediction Testing

To give a boost to your challenges of certain thoughts and, thereby, reduce their likelihood of occurring to you, it is helpful to test your predictions. *Prediction testing* is an extension of the principles that you have already learned. It is based on the realization that our thoughts and interpretations are guesses or hypotheses, not facts. An individual's interpretations represent one of several possible interpretations, and they tend to be biased in ways that depend on things like mood.

Think of specific anxiety-provoking events that could occur over the next week. Make a list of the self-statements that occur to you in anticipation of or during those situations, using the Prediction Testing Form available in your packet. For example, if you are anticipating a social event, you might identify a typical self-statement as "I am going to feel so anxious that no one will want to speak to me." After you have identified the self-statements for each situation, rate each self-statement on a 100-point scale in terms of how likely you think it is to occur. Zero means there is no chance that it will happen, 100 means it definitely will

Prediction Testing Form

See Figure 9.1 in your workbook.

```
0   10   20   30   40   50   60   70   80   90   100
No Chance         Moderate Chance         Definite Chance
```

For each event, rate the probability of your self-statement's coming true according to the scale above.

Upcoming events	Self-statements	Probability now	Did it occur? (Yes/No)
1. Lunch with friends	I'll be so anxious that I won't be able to eat.	70	No
2. Shopping in grocery store alone	I'll lose control and run out of the store.	80	No
3. Driving on highway	I'll get so disoriented that I won't find my way.	60	No

Copyright © 1994 Graywind Publications, Inc.   Mastery of Your Anxiety and Panic

Figure 9.1. Example of Prediction Testing Form

happen, and 50 means a moderate chance that it will happen. Base these ratings on how you typically feel when worrying about those events; that is, at this point do not logically evaluate the probability. Just rate how you typically feel. Then, put these lists of situations, self-statements, and ratings aside for a week.

At the end of the week, record whether the predicted events occurred. In most cases, you will find they did not. Prediction testing is another way of seeing how inaccurate thoughts can generate anxiety.

Remember that you are not estimating how anxious you will feel in a given situation. Instead, you are rating the likelihood of the feared consequence of the anxiety, such as being laughed at, going crazy, or fainting. Do not rate the likelihood of having a panic attack. As we know, a panic attack is largely the result of feared dangers such as being laughed at, going crazy, or fainting.

A specific self-statement may be "I will be too anxious to understand what John is saying to me." "Not understanding John" might be rated with a probability of 50 at the beginning of the week. After the event is over, you may protest that you did understand John, but you felt extremely anxious, and the anxiety made it harder to listen. However, the question is "Could you understand?" and that is the basis for the rating.

Examples of events that Jill anticipated and her ratings of them for each event are listed in Figure 9.1. When the week was over, Jill could see how much she had worried without real cause. Therefore, the next time she anticipated an upcoming event, she was able to challenge her predictions by recognizing that, based on her own evidence, they were unlikely.

Looking for Causes of Unexpected Panics

If you still believe that some of your panics are unexpected and you continue to be frightened because you don't know when the next one will occur, the following discussion will be useful for you. An analysis of causes involves finding all triggers of anxiety and panic. Understanding the specific trigger removes anxiety associated with uncertainty and helps to decrease the need to search for other reasons, such as being in physical danger. Also, the identification of triggers helps to develop a sense of control by removing the feeling that you are a victim of your emotions.

An important part of this analysis is the awareness that having sensations does not necessarily mean panic or anxiety; everyone has sensations at times, for natural reasons. In other words, the experience of sensations per se may seem unpredictable, from changes in hormone levels or natural biological rhythms. However, the presence of those sensations is not a panic attack unless you react to them with fear or anxiety. Remember, it is all in how you interpret the sensations.

Given your sensitivity to panic-related sensations, it is more likely that you will notice normal fluctuations that would otherwise pass unnoticed. Then, if you add fear to the cycle, those sensations are likely to intensify. The goal of this program is to reduce your fear of sensations, which will in turn reduce the intensity of the sensations when they do occur and reduce your focus of attention on those sensations.

The second major objective of an analysis of causes is to realize that all panic and anxiety are related to cues. They are reactions. Sometimes the cue is easy to identify, sometimes it is misidentified, and, at other times, it is subtle and more difficult to find. When the cue is difficult to identify, the panic seems to be unexpected. It is sometimes difficult to be aware of the reasons a pattern of behavior emerged without doing a careful analysis. This is true for all forms of behavior, including smoking, eating, and drinking. Although panic is a sudden and intense experience, the suddenness and intensity do not mean that it is spontaneous or unrelated to prior events.

There are two good examples of what seems to be unexpected panic but, in fact, is likely related to subtle cues. One is the experience of panicking from a relaxed state. The second is waking from sleep in a panic. This second type is called a *nocturnal panic attack*. About half of the people who suffer from panic disorder have at least one nocturnal panic attack. About 20% of this same group have repeated nocturnal panic attacks.

It is normal to have fluctuations in physiological rhythms during the night. Also, the more anxious an individual is in general, the more likely it is that the person's physical responding accelerates at different points during sleep. That is, heart rate and respiration can increase at times. If these changes occur with an increase in level of consciousness during sleep (as happens sometimes between sleep stages), then the individual may awaken. If someone is sensitive to and frightened by sensations, it is understandable that these changes, combined with the disorientation of waking, can lead to a panic reaction. General anxiety is often related to restless sleep and awakenings as well. However, someone who is generally anxious (but is not fearful of panic sensations) is more likely to respond to the wakenings with frustration than with fear and panic. Thus, waking in a panic attack is not an unexplainable event.

Deep relaxation is also associated with sudden fear. Deep relaxation entails dwelling on oneself, or body scanning, and noticing normal sensations. These same sensations might not be noticed if your attention is focused elsewhere. Some people also experience a feeling of loss of control when they relax deeply. So, again, fear emerges in reaction to experiencing or noticing scary bodily sensations that occur, in this case, from deep relaxation.

It is likely that you have times when you have expected episodes of anxiety or panic. That is, you might expect to feel anxious or panicky in situations where you have felt anxious before, such as shopping malls, being alone at home, or

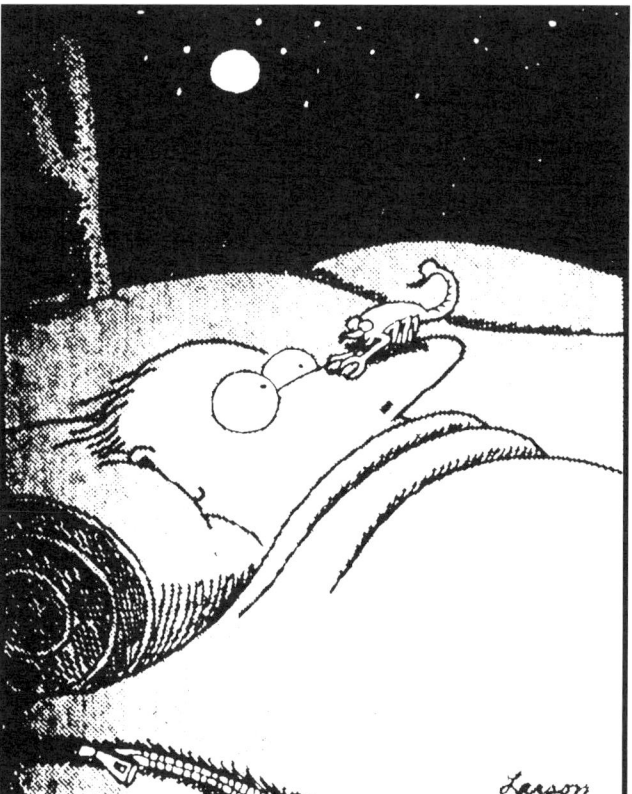

"Excuse me, but the others sent me up here to ask you not to roll around so much."

driving a car. Times when you unexpectedly become anxious or panic may be related to the following, more subtle cues:

Physical State

- Feeling natural sensations that have been associated with anxiety or panic in the past and, therefore, can trigger anxiety when noticed. Examples are breathlessness or increased heart rate from physical exercise; nausea from overeating, "bad food," alcohol, or ill health; or feeling hot from the sun.

- Feeling natural sensations that have not been associated with anxiety or panic in the past but that are interpreted as signs of anxiety or panic. For example, fatigue, hunger, thirst, frustration, and anger have sometimes been misinterpreted as signs of anxiety and, therefore, begin the spiral into panic.

- Feeling sensations that are due to high levels of arousal, such as muscle tension, racing heart, sweating, and trembling.

Thoughts

Thoughts are not only important after the anxious cycle has begun but can also trigger anxious feelings. For example, worrying about one's ability to cope with anxiety, thinking about the possibility of panicking again, and worrying about upcoming events can all serve as triggers. Remember, whenever a person perceives threat (even if no real threat exists), the body responds with changes in preparation for the threat. Those changes lead to the experience of sensations, which in turn may be misinterpreted. As a result, fear escalates.

General Stressors

Subtle pressures, both positive and negative, can add to a feeling of anxiety or panic. For example, dealing with hostile people, being caught in heavy traffic, meeting a deadline, or going on a date can all serve as triggers to panic.

Over the next week, spend time evaluating the likely triggers each time you feel anxious or panicky. Review this list to determine whether any of those elements were involved in your anxiety or fear reaction.

Exercise

Continue to monitor your anxiety and panic using the Daily Mood Record and Panic Attack Record. Continue to use relaxation training, breathing control, or both when feeling anxious and tense. Continue to challenge overestimations and catastrophic self-statements each time you feel anxious or panicky or, at least, at the end of each day by reviewing your episodes of anxiety and panic. For each episode, also determine the triggers using the previous list. Continue this exercise for a full week before proceeding to the next chapter.

Self-Assessment

Answer by circling **T** (True) or **F** (False). Answers are provided in Appendix A.

1. The experience of an unexpected panic is an indication that the trigger was not obvious. **T   F**

2. Unexpected panic attacks are more threatening than those that are expected. **T   F**

3. If you do not successfully apply methods of relaxation or breathing, then you are in dire trouble.   **T F**

4. Situations are not the only triggers of panic; other cues that are more subtle include physical sensations, thoughts, and general stressors.   **T F**

5. Self-statement modification, when it is used, should lead to an immediate reduction of physical sensations during a panic attack.   **T F**

Chapter 10

Producing the Panic Sensations

Review

Review your last week's Daily Mood and Panic Attack Records and add the information to your Progress Record Form. Think about patterns that developed. Do you understand each episode of anxiety or panic in terms of the behavioral, thought, and physical response components and sequencing? Do you understand your emotional reactions? Also, record your judgments of probability and ability to cope on your Self-Statement Rating Form. Have your estimates changed?

Response Component Strategies

Review your use of either breathing control or relaxation and self-statement modification over the preceding week. Ensure that you are using the strategies when tension or anxiety are first noticed. Also, remember not to use these in a desperate way, as if they are needed to prevent a dire consequence such as dying, losing control, or being made fun of by others. Even if you are unable to slow down your breathing or to control your muscle tension, you will still survive.

Review in your mind the way in which you have been using the self-statement modification techniques. Sometimes, the self-statement challenges can become distractors. As distractors, they do not aid in learning to be less fearful but, instead, just help you to get through the immediate event. For example, compare someone who says, "It will be okay, I'm fully in control, nothing bad will happen," to someone who says, "What am I afraid of? I'm afraid of fainting. How likely is it that I will faint, given the fact that I have felt this way so many times before and have never fainted? I know that I tend to overestimate the risk of fainting when I feel this way. The feelings will pass." The first person is using the self-statement challenges as a quick fix, which does not really work in the long run. The second person is examining her or his thoughts and looking at the alternatives on the basis of real evidence. The first person is using the challenges to fend against fear instead of changing his or her perception to remove the motivation for fear.

Also, check your predictions from the past week on the Prediction Testing Form. Were they accurate? If the things you worried about did not occur, your prediction was inaccurate. An example might be that you were able to drive despite feeling dizzy, or you were able to walk through the mall despite feeling lightheaded. Now make a new set of predictions for events that will occur during the next week and record them on the Prediction Testing Form. Remember to base your ratings on how you usually feel in those situations. (That is, do not use logical analyses for these ratings, because the goal is to see how accurate your initial predictions are.)

Finally, review your attempts to conduct an analysis of causes for each time you felt anxious or panicky. Did you at least analyze causes at the end of the day for all episodes? Were you able to identify possible cues that explained the panic spiral even though it seemed unexpected at first? Were there subtle physical sensations of which you became aware? Did you have thoughts that started off the spiral? Were there stressors that made you feel more anxious and, in turn, more aware of the possibility of panic and more sensitive to small physical changes?

Repeated Practice With Panic Sensations—Why?

As you know by now, fearful reactions to sensations are central to panic. You have been learning how to manage your fear by changing what you tell yourself about the sensations and by learning to slow down the physical sensations. Now, you will learn to confront the sensations directly.

As a first step, you must identify which sensations remain scary to you. To do this, you will go through a series of exercises that bring on sensations similar to those caused by anxiety and panic. For example, some of the exercises bring on a racing heart, whereas others lead to dizziness. Still others bring on feelings of unreality. After identifying which sensations are still fearful, your next step is to practice experiencing those sensations repeatedly in order to lessen their fearfulness. This process is called exposure, or confronting feared objects or situations to become less fearful.

At first, it may seem strange to make yourself feel the very things, the sensations, that you already experience too much. However, exposure sensations are different from the sensations you feel naturally. Exposure therapy means that you bring on feared sensations and experience them long enough for learning to take place, specifically, learning that you are safe and that the sensations will not harm you. This learning of safety leads to fear reduction. On the other hand, you probably still respond to naturally occurring feared sensations by avoiding them. By trying to stop them as soon as possible, by going home, seeking help, and so on, you do not learn that the sensations are not really dangerous. So, you will be doing the opposite of what you normally do. Instead of trying to escape from sensations, you will be encouraging the experience of sensations. After some relatively artificial exercises here, in the next chapter, you will engage in activities that in and of themselves produce sensations.

In other words, repeated exposure to feared sensations is like overcoming a fear of other things by repeated practice. For example, people who are afraid of speaking in public benefit from just getting up in front of a group of people and speaking, over and over again. If you were afraid of an animal, you could lessen your fear by repeatedly getting closer to it. In fact, you might have already had this type of experience. It often happens when people first learn to drive. The first few drives can be very scary, but gradually driving becomes easy and natural. Skiing is another example. At first, it is frightening to go at fast speeds down a slippery slope, but with practice, you turn your fear into excitement and pleasure. Think of a fear that you have lessened through repeated exposure.

Why does repeated practice lessen fearfulness? It is believed that there are two main reasons. First, by becoming familiar with the object or situation, the person becomes less uncertain about what could happen. Associated with this decreased uncertainty is a decrease in arousal due to the fear. In addition, with repeated practice, the individual corrects his or her misperception of danger. That is, repeated practice reduces the fear. In this way, the repeated exposure expands on the work you have been doing with your self-statements. Self-statement modification and exposure fit together well because they both correct the misperception of danger. Of course, if the sensations really were dangerous, then it would not be safe to induce them. But they are not dangerous.

In addition, the sensation induction exercises will let you use the breathing, relaxation, and self-statement strategies you have learned. Although you should still use these strategies when you feel anxious, using them during these exposure practices will make them easier to use in your daily life. That is, the more you rehearse a strategy, the more powerful and natural it becomes.

Identifying Which Sensations Are Fearful

Now, proceed through the following list of exercises. The goal is to identify any sensations that you feel as a result of each exercise. Once you have identified the sensations, rate three different aspects: first, the intensity of the sensations (rated on an 8-point scale, where 0 means not at all, and 8 means extreme); second, the level of anxiety or fear you experience in response to the sensations (rated on an 8-point scale, where 0 means none at all, and 8 means extreme); and, third, how similar those sensations are to the ones you would feel in a natural episode of anxiety or panic (rated on an 8-point scale, where 0 means not at all similar, and 8 means exactly the same). These ratings are made on the Sensation Induction Record. If you are working with a doctor or mental health professional, he or she can demonstrate each exercise for you. Otherwise, try each one at home. For your own comfort, we recommend having someone with you the first time you do these exercises; however, a companion is not necessary because the effects produced by the exercises, like those of a panic attack, are harmless and will subside.

- Shake your head loosely from side to side for 30 seconds (to produce dizziness or disorientation).

- Place your head between your legs for 30 seconds and then lift it quickly (to produce lightheadedness or blood rushing).

- Take one step up, using stairs, a box, or a footstool, and immediately step down. Do this repeatedly for 1 minute at a rate fast enough so you notice your heart beating quickly (to produce racing heart and shortness of breath).

- Hold your breath for as long as you can or for about 30–45 seconds (to produce chest tightness, and smothering feelings).

- Tense every part of your body for 1 minute without causing pain. Tense your arms, legs, stomach, back, shoulders, face—everything. Alternatively, try holding a push-up position for one minute or for as long as you can (to produce muscle tension, weakness, and trembling).

- Spin in a chair for 1 minute. (A chair that spins, such as a desk chair, is ideal. It is even better if someone is there to spin you around. Otherwise, stand up and turn around quickly to make yourself dizzy. Be near a soft chair or couch that you can sit in after 1 minute is up. This exercise will produce dizziness and perhaps nausea as well.

- Hyperventilate for 1 minute. As described in Chapter 5, breathe deeply and fast, using a lot of force. Sit down as you do this. This exercise might produce unreality, shortness of breath, tingling, cold or hot feelings, dizziness, or headache.

- Breathe through a thin straw for 1 minute. Do not allow any air through your nose; hold your nostrils together (to produce feelings of restricted air flow or smothering).

- Stare at a small spot on the wall or stare at yourself in the mirror for 2 minutes. Stare as hard as you can to produce feelings of unreality.

Other exercises can be designed to suit your own patterns. For example, if you are most distressed by visual distortions, try looking at a light for 30 seconds and then looking at a blank wall to see the after-image. If you focus on throat sensations, put pressure against the sides of your throat or press down on the back of your tongue. If you worry about choking, spend 1 minute just focusing on the sensation of swallowing. Another exercise is to sit in a hot, stuffy room or car for 5 minutes. You should know by now which sensations scare you most, so be creative and invent some ways to produce them. You need to experience the sensations most important for you.

Here are Jill's responses to each of the standard exercises. The ratings for intensity, anxiety, and similarity are in parentheses and are taken from her Sensation Induction Record (see Figure 10.1).

- Head Shaking

    "Wow—that makes me feel dizzy and disoriented. My eyes are out of focus—but they are, as I speak, coming back into focus." For Jill, this exercise did not produce much fear (2), nor were the sensations rated as being very similar to her natural anxiety or panic sensations (2). Nevertheless, she rated the sensations at the end of the procedure as quite intense (6).

- Head Lift

    "I feel a little dizzy—and lightheaded. This was not much at all." She did not report any fear (1) or much similarity (2) and rated the sensation intensity as being quite mild (3).

- Step Ups (Jill stopped this one after 45 seconds.)

    "I feel like I have to stop—my heart is beating fast, and I feel sweaty and out of breath. Usually, I try to avoid doing any exercise." Jill rated this procedure as producing sensations that were very intense (7), very similar to what she felt during her panic attacks (6), and, initially, as quite frightening (5).

- Breath Holding

    "Nothing—just a little chest pressure." Jill's ratings were all mild (2).

- Complete Tension

    "I feel a little shaky and trembly and weak." Although the sensations were quite intense for Jill (5), she did not fear them (1) and rated the similarity as being low (1).

- Spinning (Jill stopped this after 30 seconds.)

    "Boy, I feel really dizzy. The room is spinning—I am spinning. And my heart is racing and I feel sweaty. It's calming down now." These sensations were very intense (7), similar to those she felt when she panicked (5), and frightening (4).

Sensation Induction Record

See Figure 10.1 in your workbook.

0	1	2	3	4	5	6	7	8
None		**Mild**		**Moderate**		**Strong**		**Extreme**

For each exercise, rate your anxiety, sensation intensity, and similarity to panic according to the scale above. Then mark a star for each exercise that rated 3 or above in the similarity column. Finally, rank the starred exercises by level of anxiety.

Exercise	Intensity	Anxiety	Similarity	Star	Rank
Head shaking	6	2	2		
Head lift	3	1	2		
Step-ups	7	5	6	*	3
Breath holding	2	2	2		
Tension	5	1	1		
Spinning	7	4	5	*	1
Hyperventilation	7	6	5	*	4
Straw	6	6	4	*	5
Staring	5	4	5	*	2
Others					

Copyright © 1994 Graywind Publications, Inc.   Mastery of Your Anxiety and Panic

Figure 10.1. Example of Sensation Induction Record

- Hyperventilating (Jill stopped after 45 seconds.)

    "I feel really hot and sweaty, tingly in my face, lightheaded and like I need to take a deep breath." Again, this procedure produced sensations that Jill rated as being very intense (7), similar to her natural panics (5) and frightening (6).

- Straw Breathing (Jill stopped after 35 seconds.)

    "I feel like I can't keep going, I have to take a deep breath." Jill rated the symptoms as being intense (6), similar to her panic symptoms (4), and frightening (6).

- Staring

    "This is weird. It feels a bit like the spacy feelings I get when I'm just coming out of a panic attack. I don't like this at all." Jill rated the symptoms as being moderate to intense (5), similar to her panic symptoms (5) and moderately fearful (4).

Now, try each exercise. Go as long as is specified for each exercise. Of course, you can stop before then if you feel you must. Use the Sensation Induction Record in your packet of forms to list the sensations and to record ratings of intensity, similarity, and fear.

Now, look at your list of responses in your Sensation Induction Record. Place a star (*) next to the exercises that produced symptoms you rated as at least 3 on the 8-point scale of similarity. Next, rank the starred exercises in order of the level of anxiety. Your repeated-exposure practices will begin with the exercise that was least frightening but which has a similarity rating of at least 3. So, Jill's exercises were ranked (from most to least fearful) as follows: first, spinning; second, staring; third, step ups; fourth, hyperventilating; and fifth, straw breathing.

When an exercise is rated as producing at least some anxiety, it means that there is still fear of the sensations, which has not been completely removed by self-statement modification and breathing control or relaxation. It also shows a need to do more work to overcome the fear through the next steps of repeated exposure. Finally, it suggests that you are likely to be fearful of sensations that occur naturally.

If these exercises do not produce any anxiety, it is important to explore the reasons that they do not.

- Is it because none of the sensations of which you are fearful were produced by these exercises? If so, then be creative and come up with others that produce the sensations relevant to your fears.

- Did you stop the exercise too soon in anticipation of strong sensations? For example, you might have stopped spinning after 10 seconds because you were just starting to feel off balance but you did not spin long enough to be very fearful. If so, then repeat the exercise and try to do it for a longer time.

- Have you truly overcome your fears of sensations as a result of the work you have done so far? If so, we still recommend that you continue with the repeated exposures, because overlearning is helpful in the long run. Exposure therapy is a bit like taking penicillin even after the symptoms of infection have gone.

- Is it because you feel safe in the setting in which you performed the exercise or with the person who was there with you? Some of our clients have noted that if they had to do the exercises alone, they would be more frightened. When accompanied, they feel safe because there would be help if something went wrong. Note that this fear is based on a belief that they would indeed be in danger if they had the sensations when alone. In fact, these exercises are no more dangerous when you are alone than when you are accompanied. If this is the reason for lack of fear, then try the exercises alone or away from help.

You might say to yourself that because you know where the sensations are coming from, that is, the exercise, and because you know that the sensations will go away when the exercise is stopped, the sensations are not frightening. This reason is okay as long as you can say the same about sensations that occur naturally. That is, you no longer fear naturally occurring sensations because there is always a reason for them, and you know that they will pass. However, if you are still fearful of natural sensations but not of the exercise-induced sensations, you probably still view naturally occurring sensations as threatening. If so, reread Chapters 4, 7, 8, and 9. This review will remind you of what the sensations represent, where they come from, the realization that they are not dangerous, and the fact that they will not last forever. In either case, continue with the sensation-induction procedures because building nonfearful responses will help you when you feel the sensations naturally.

Finally, you might not be fearful of the sensations because they are not occurring in a "dangerous" context. Sometimes people are fearful of sensations only when they occur in a certain place, such as at social events, when speaking in front of groups, or when driving on the freeway. If so, we recommend that you continue with the sensation induction procedures anyway, because building nonfearful responses to the sensations will help you when you encounter them in the specific situations. The Agoraphobia Supplement will also help you to confront the sensations in the situations.

By the way, the last three listed reasons all illustrate the role of thoughts. That is, the sensations are the same no matter how they are brought on. The way you react to them, however, may differ and depends on whether you think the sensations are more or less dangerous because you are alone or accompanied, because they seem predictable and controllable, or because you are in a given situation.

Repeated Practice With Bodily Sensations

For the repeated practice of each exercise, a timer, such as a stopwatch or watch, is helpful. Follow these steps:

1. Choose the least anxiety-provoking exercise from the starred (*) items that you identified on the Sensation Induction Record. If you were not fearful of any exercise but are doing repeated practice anyway, then just go through each exercise in the order listed in this chapter.

2. Conduct the exercise in the following ways:

    - Continue the exercise for at least 30 seconds after the point at which you first notice sensations or for 10 seconds in the case of holding your breath. This is important. By continuing to feel the sensations, you are breaking the tendency to escape from them right away. If you stopped the exercise as soon as you felt the sensation, then you would only be reinforcing what you do normally, which is to fear and avoid the feelings.

    - Try to produce the sensations as strongly as you can. Do not avoid the sensations by doing the exercise with hesitation or mildly. Do not be too cautious. Experiencing the sensations intensely is crucial. For example, for the spinning exercise, the turning must be continuous so that dizziness comes on. When hyperventilating, ensure that the air is forced out with a lot of pressure and the breathing rate is fast. You will defeat the purpose of the exercise if you do not try really hard.

    - Do not become distracted during the procedure. Remain focused on what you are feeling. Keep an objective focus of attention at all times.

    - After tolerating the sensations for the length of time specified, stop the exercise and then rate the intensity of your anxiety or fear on the 8-point scale, using the Exposure Exercise Record included in your packet of MAP–II Monitoring Forms. ("Trial" refers to whether this is the first, second, third time, and so on, that you have done this exercise.) Anxiety or fear is rated in terms of the highest level you felt during the exercise or right after you stopped.

    - Then, use breathing control or relaxation, identify negative self-statements, and challenge those self-statements. This step is where you get to practice your strategies. Be aware of negative statements

"It's OK! It's OK! The tunnel was closing in on me there for a while, but I'm all right now."

such as "I have to stop—I can't tolerate these feelings." That is a prediction you are making, which is based on fear only. You can, in fact, tolerate and continue the procedures. Ask yourself what is the worst that can happen and what is the likelihood of dying, going crazy, or losing control? Examine the negative predictions you are making about the sensations becoming more intense or lasting longer or their effects on the rest of your day. Then, go through each prediction and question the evidence. This section of the repeated exposure is particularly important. If you conduct the exercises repeatedly but maintain the belief that you are continuing to place yourself in danger or that it is only with great relief that you made it through, then you will not benefit fully.

- Do not apply the strategies before or during the exercise. It is important to feel the sensations fully. This instruction may seem contradictory to what you have done so far—to use the strategies as soon as you noticed symptoms or anxiety. However, now it is time to experience the symptoms fully and to use the strategies only afterwards.

3. Repeat the points in Step 2 for the same exercise as many times as needed to reduce your anxiety or fear level to 2 or less on the 8-point scale. Wait until your symptoms have abated and you no longer feel anxious before you repeat the exercise. If your anxiety or fear does not reduce to 2 after five trials, then stop practicing and start again the next day. Otherwise, you will just exhaust yourself.

4. After your anxiety has reduced to 2 or less for a given exercise, move to the next most anxiety provoking exercise. Use the same steps for this and the rest of the exercises.

5. Practice repeated exposure to one exercise daily, up to five times per exercise. You might need only three practices for a given exercise in order to be less fearful. You can then move on to the next exercise or start a new one the next day.

A partial example of Jill's Exposure Exercise Record is presented in Figure 10.2, showing when each exercise had been practiced enough. She practiced the following exercises:

- Spinning
- Staring
- Step Ups
- Hyperventilating
- Straw Breathing

In the clinic, like most of our clients, Jill found that her anxiety levels quickly reduced. The third time she spun, she stated that the sensations were still intense, but she was only mildly fearful. She even spun for a longer time. The fourth time, her anxiety rating was only 2. When she first practiced alone, the fear was a little higher (4 the first time). However, the fear reduced as she kept practicing alone.

At first, Jill would anxiously wait for the dizziness to abate after spinning, and so she added tension and prolonged the symptoms. However, after a couple of days of practicing five times each day, she realized the symptoms were tolerable, and so they decreased. This point is important. If you notice that you anxiously wait for the symptoms to subside, pay attention to your negative thoughts. If you are truly nonfearful, it does not matter how long the sensations take to subside. Waiting for them to subside means that you still have some concerns about losing control, collapsing, and so on.

Exposure Exercise Record

See Figure 10.2 in your workbook.

0	1	2	3	4	5	6	7	8
None		**Mild**		**Moderate**		**Strong**		**Extreme**

Write each exercise you practice. For each trial, rate your anxiety/fear according to the scale above.

Day	Exercise	Trial	Anxiety/Fear
Day 1	Spinning (accompanied)	1	6
	"	2	5
	"	3	3
	"	4	2
Day 2	Spinning (alone)	1	4
	"	2	3
	"	3	2
	"	4	1
	"	5	1
Day 3	Step-ups	1	5
	"	2	4
	"	3	2
Day 4	Hyperventilation	1	6
	"	2	6
	"	3	5
	"	4	5
	"	5	4
Day 5	Hyperventilation	1	5
	"	2	4
	"	3	4
	"	4	3

Copyright © 1994 Graywind Publications, Inc.   Mastery of Your Anxiety and Panic

Figure 10.2. Example (Partial) of Exposure Exercise Record

Jill practiced hyperventilating for 2 days, because at first she felt that she could not tolerate the symptoms. It was important for her to learn that although the symptoms were not comfortable, they were not unbearable and could be tolerated.

As with many people, Jill's anxiety or fear levels were a little higher after going several days without practice. That pattern is nothing to be worried about. It just shows the need for more practice.

Keep in the mind the goal of these exercises. By learning to be less fearful of sensations produced in this way, you are doing several things:

- You gain more evidence to support the notion that these sensations are not dangerous.

- You build a response pattern that is nonfearful, so that when you feel sensations in your daily life, you will have this new response to draw on. In other words, the new nonfearful response will be automatic instead of the old fearful one.

- You gain confidence in your ability to tolerate these types of sensations.

As a result of these first three results, the sensations will occur less often in your daily life, because by learning to be less afraid of them, the anxiety about their recurrence lessens as well. Remember, the only reason to anxiously await an event is if you fear it.

Exercise

Do each of these over the next 7 days.

- Continue to use breathing control or relaxation or both upon awareness of tension, anxiety or panic.

- Continue to identify and modify anxiety-provoking self-statements. Perform this analysis at the end of each day but also use it when you are anxious or panicky.

- Continue an analysis of causes of anxiety and panic episodes.

- Practice daily the exercises that were conducted in this session. Do not put this off—Practice every day if you want to get the most benefit. Repeat a single exercise as many times as needed to experience a level of maximum anxiety or fear no greater than 2. Record your levels of anxiety on the Exposure Exercise Record. Read the instructions in this chapter carefully to make sure you do these correctly.

Self-Assessment

Answer by circling **T** (True) or **F** (False). Answers are provided in Appendix A.

1. It is important to experience the sensations to the fullest and to allow the anxiety to be experienced fully when you practice the various exercises. **T F**

2. All individuals respond in exactly the same way to these exercises. **T F**

3. Repeat the exercises as many times as necessary for the level of anxiety to reduce to a 2 on the 8-point scale. **T F**

4. Try to prevent the anxiety from developing before you do the exercises by applying breathing retraining and self-statement modification. **T F**

Chapter 11

Producing Panic Sensations in Your Daily Life

Review

Review your Daily Mood and Panic Attack Records. Add the average anxiety and number of panic attacks to your Progress Record Form. Review your use of breathing control or relaxation and self-statement modification. Did you examine each panic and anxiety episode using a step-by-step sequential analysis? What about your predictions? Check your Prediction Testing Form. How accurate were you last week? What can you learn from this? Have your estimates changed? Add your judgments of probability and ability to cope to your Self-Statement Rating Form. Are you more confident in your ability to cope or are you less worried about certain things happening?

Did you practice daily the exercises introduced in the previous chapter? Did you notice changes in the level of anxiety or fear with repeated practice? Did you conduct the exercises as described or did you avoid them? It is important that you produce the sensations fully. Did you distract yourself while you were bringing on the sensations, such as thinking about other events? If so, stop this because it prevents the benefit of the exposure. You must experience everything to the fullest in order to benefit from this procedure.

Continued Exposure Exercise

Continue working on your list of sensation-induction exercises. Practice the exercise until you notice the sensations. Remember to continue the exercise for at least 30 seconds longer, or 10 seconds in the case of holding your breath, after the sensations are first noticed. Record the intensity of the anxiety or fear on your exposure exercise record. Then apply your strategies, that is, breathing control, relaxation, and self-statement modification, to reduce the fear and anxiety. Once you feel calm, repeat the exercise. Do this as many times as needed for the maximum anxiety or fear rating to reach 2 or less. Then continue with the next exercise. Continue in this way until you have gone through all of the exercises.

Remember to include the exercises most relevant for you. Do not leave out the most frightening exercises. These are the exercises that are most important to do.

Use the Exposure Exercise Record form to monitor your progress. Do not worry if it takes more than 1 or 2 days to feel comfortable with an exercise. Sometimes exposure goes quickly, and sometimes it takes a while. Either fast or slow, it works, so keep trying. Pay attention to the kinds of negative thoughts you have that might slow the rate of fear reduction. For example, if you believe that you could really faint by hyperventilating for 2 minutes, then you will remain fearful of this. In truth, the chances of fainting are small, unless you faint very easily in many situations. Even if you are a fainter, the chances are still tiny.

Do not do any more than five trials on any one day. Remember to separate unpleasantness from fear. Although feeling dizzy may never be pleasant for you, it can be tolerated without fear. If none of the exercises produces a level of fear greater than 2 by the middle of the week, just repeat each one twice each day.

Continue this practice over the next week.

Activities Exposure

The next step is to use the same kind of approach to natural activities that induce sensations similar to those you get during panic. You might avoid some activities because they produce sensations. Examples include: drinking coffee (because of the stimulant effect), eating chocolate (because of the stimulant or expected stimulant effect), aerobic activity (because of the cardiovascular effect), lifting heavy objects or doing an anaerobic activity (because of the heightened blood pressure and dizziness effects), moving body position quickly, running up flights of stairs, being in hot and stuffy rooms, closing the door while having a shower, taking saunas, watching horror movies, having sexual relations, walking outside in cold air, walking outside in intense heat, hiking, doing sports, eating heavy meals, and so on.

Examine these and similar activities (shown in the list below) and assess whether you have been avoiding them or doing them but with hesitation and fear. This is a good example of the way in which sensations can cue panic attacks even though they are not seen as a reason for panicking (analysis of causes). In the next chapter, you will begin practicing these. Prepare yourself for this by listing all activities you have avoided or felt afraid of because of the sensations.

Daily Activities That Produce Panic Sensations

- Running up flights of stairs
- Walking outside in intense heat
- Hot, stuffy rooms
- Hot, stuffy cars
- Hot, stuffy stores or shopping malls
- Walking outside in very cold weather
- Aerobics
- Lifting heavy objects
- Dancing
- Sexual relations
- Watching horror movies
- Eating heavy meals
- Watching exciting movies or sports events
- Getting involved in "heated" debates
- Having showers with the doors and windows closed
- Having a sauna
- Hiking
- Sports
- Drinking coffee, caffeinated beverages
- Eating chocolate
- Standing quickly from a sitting position
- Getting angry

What to Do if Anxiety and Panic Recur

It is common for anxiety and panic to recur from time to time during treatment. The return of panic is more likely under times of stress. As described earlier, stress increases tension and arousal, which lead to increased symptoms. Stress might also facilitate old ways of fearful responding.

It is important not to confuse the return of panic with treatment failure. This recurrence is just a sign that the anxious thoughts, tendency to overbreathe, physical tension, and sensitivity to sensations are still there. The strategies for reducing sensations and modifying your thoughts are designed to break the response cycle of fear and panic. They are not "Band-Aid" techniques that cover underlying panic; they are strategies that disintegrate the experience of panic. Also, repeated exposures to the sensations will reduce your sensitivity so that when different sensations arise, fear is much less likely to occur and your awareness of those sensations, in general, will reduce. This, in turn, will reduce your level of general anxiety and thereby decrease the chances of having sensations in the first place.

However, you might still experience times of intense anxiety and panic, especially in new or demanding situations where it is easier to revert to old habits. It is important to put a recurrence into perspective. It is not a sign of failure or relapse but a signal that there is still work to be done. This is normal, as it is any time one learns a new set of skills. Progress through treatment is rarely steady. However, the times of panic allow more learning to take place. So, believe it or not, having panics can be helpful for your treatment.

You might feel that it is harder to use the strategies when you are very anxious. That is true.

However, there are key things to do that help you maintain a more objective focus rather than being caught up in the cycle of fear. That is, management at this level still requires interruption of the cycle of the emotional response.

The following are the kinds of problems that may be experienced at points of high anxiety and panic:

- The panic is so sudden that I do not have time to think.
- I feel so distraught that I cannot think clearly or logically.
- At the times when I am feeling very panicky, it is hard to believe the challenging self-statements and my belief in the negative statements increases, that is, I really am going to die.
- I just cannot control my physical tension or breathing patterns.

Determine if these or other fear processes occur at times of intense fear and panic and make it harder to use your skills. For each one, here are the key points to remember:

- Ask yourself a series of key questions to help you become more objective, such as "What are my thoughts?" "What is the worst that can happen?" "What is the likelihood of that happening?" "What was the trigger to this episode?" "How have my reactions spiraled into the feeling of panic?" and so forth.
- Remember that despite the feeling that what you are most afraid of will occur, for example, losing control, or something catastrophic, this

feeling will pass. It comes from a set of inaccurate beliefs, and the same fears have come up before yet have not happened.

- Continue to try to reduce the sensations by breathing control or relaxation. Remember, even if you feel that you cannot control your breathing or your physical tension, the symptoms are harmless anyway.

- Write the important points on a small card that can be carried with you and used as a prompt when you are panicky. This will help you to become an objective observer of the sequence of events, which in turn allows you to be more in control of your reactions.

Exercise

Over the next 7 days, do the following:

- Continue the use of breathing control or relaxation training, self-statement modification, and analysis of causes.

- Practice daily the sensation-induction exercises with repetition of each exercise until the anxiety or fear is reduced to a level of .2. During these exercises, experience the sensations to the fullest before applying your strategies. Record your reactions to each exercise on the Sensation Induction Record Form.

- Identify activities that you avoid or that you engage in with fear because they bring on sensations that remind you of the feeling of panic.

- Use several key prompting questions and statements at times when you feel extremely panicky. Write these on a card to be carried with you.

Self-Assessment

Answer by circling **T** (True) or **F** (False). Answers are provided in Appendix A.

1. Experiencing panic at this point means that I am seriously ill or that I've lost everything that I had gained.   **T   F**

2. I must remember to ask myself key questions at times when the fear level is intense.   **T   F**

3. I should try to fight off the feeling of fear at all cost.   **T   F**

4. The more I practice the exercises, the more benefit I will get from the treatment.   **T   F**

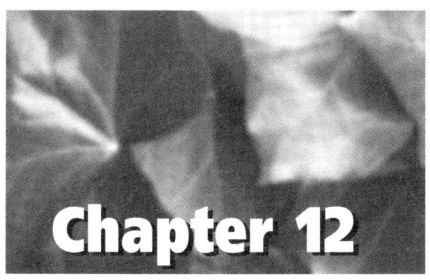

Chapter 12

Producing Panic Sensations in Your Daily Life—Continued

Review

Review your Daily Mood and Panic Attack Records and add the average anxiety and number of panic attacks to your Progress Record Form. Review your use of breathing control, relaxation, self-statement modification and analysis of causes. What about your estimates of the probability that terrible things will happen or that you will not be able to cope? Add your estimates for this week to your Self-Statement Rating Form. Look at changes in your estimates.

Did you practice bringing on sensations each day? Did your level of fear reduce in response to each exercise? Did you progress up the list of exercises until you could do each one with little anxiety? Did you question and challenge negative thoughts that arose as you induced the sensations? Did you slow down your breathing or relax after the exercise was over? If you have not completed your exercises, it is better to wait until you have before moving on to the activities in this chapter.

Were you able to use the questions and key statements (written on a card) at times when you felt extreme anxiety or panic? A main point to remember is that fear in and of itself is harmless and that even if you did nothing, it would go away on its own.

Confrontation With Fear in Your Daily Life—General Issues

Did you identify activities you have avoided or feared because of the sensations they produce? Examples include caffeine, aerobic exercise, and hot rooms. If not, then look at the list in Chapter 11 to come up with your own list.

Activities Hierarchy

See Figure 12.1 in your workbook.

0	1	2	3	4	5	6	7	8
None		**Mild**		**Moderate**		**Strong**		**Extreme**

List activities in order from least difficult to most difficult. For each activity, rate your current anxiety according to the scale above.

Activity	Current anxiety
1. Eating chocolate	2
2. Watching exciting movies or sporting events	2
3. Eating heavy meals	3
4. Walking outside in intense heat	5
5. Hot, stuffy cars	6
6. Running up flights of stairs	7
7. Aerobics	7
8.	
9.	
10.	

Copyright © 1994 Graywind Publications, Inc.   Mastery of Your Anxiety and Panic

Figure 12.1. **Example of Activities Hierarchy Form**

Use your Activities Hierarchy Form to rank all of your activities in terms of how much anxiety or fear you feel in each (see the example in Figure 12.1). This is now your hierarchy and, as with the exercises you have been doing over the last few weeks, the goal is to repeat each activity as many times as needed to reduce anxiety to mild or lower levels. This step takes a lot of work because often these activities take more time than to do the other exercises.

Remember that the more you put into doing these practices, the more you will benefit. A friend or family member may be able to help with motivation. For example, a friend might agree to work out with you at a local gym or go out dancing or participate in sports. If you ask someone to help out, it is a good idea to tell them what you are doing and why. It also helps to tell them how they can best help you should you become anxious, that is, what they can say and do. This information can prevent them from feeling at a loss or from making the situation worse. Specific ways of involving others in exposure practices are detailed in the Agoraphobia Supplement. In general, however, we have found that involving a willing partner is helpful.

As with the other exercises, begin with the least difficult item. Make sure that you plan in advance exactly how you are going to do the task, for how long, and at what time. For example, perhaps your task is to have a shower with the windows and doors closed so that the room fills up with steam. In the past you might have avoided this situation because the steam led you to feel a sense of suffocation. So, the plan might be to close the doors and windows before you turn on the water, run the hot water for a few minutes before you get into the shower, and then stay in the shower for a specified period of time, such as 10 minutes, even if you feel a sense of suffocation. Remember, a sense of suffocation does not mean that you are indeed suffocating. Then, you get out of the shower and dry off in the steamy room for a couple of minutes before you open the door. As before, continue with the practice even if you feel sensations. If you open the doors of the shower room as soon as you feel a sense of suffocation, then you are preventing corrective learning from taking place and reinforcing the fear.

Consider another example. Your plan is to drink a cup of coffee. Because this is a frightening task, you decide to do it in steps. The first step is to drink a full cup of decaffeinated coffee (because usually you avoid even the small amount of caffeine in decaffeinated brews) at a time when someone else is around. The next step might be to drink a decaffeinated coffee alone. The next step might then be to drink a mixture of decaffeinated and caffeinated coffee, when your safe person is around, followed by drinking the same drink alone. Finally, you move on to drinking a full cup of caffeinated coffee alone.

Consider one more example. You decide to overcome your sensitivity to hot, stuffy areas. In the past, you have avoided wearing heavy clothes, especially in crowded places such as bars or malls. So, your goal is to wear a coat or a thick sweater in an already warm mall. Your first step is to find the right clothing and, perhaps, to have a couple of practices with just the heavy clothing in front of a heater at home. Then, you find a friend or family member who agrees to go to a mall or club where you can practice wearing the same clothes.

From these examples, you can see the need to be creative in coming up with the most effective practices. By this time, you are probably fully aware of your fears and avoidant behaviors and what kind of steps are best to reach your goals. So, take this on as a challenge or a problem to be solved, using all of the skills and knowledge you have learned to date.

Confrontation with Fear in Your Daily Life—Specifics

After each practice on a given activity, record the level of maximum anxiety or fear using the same form as was used for the sensation exercises (the Exposure Exercise Record). After rating your anxiety, use relaxation or breathing control and self-statement modification.

When you feel calm, repeat the activity. The repetition can be done either right after the first practice or after some delay, depending on the activity. For example, sitting in a hot, stuffy room can be repeated fairly quickly, but eating certain foods may take longer. Similarly, although you can practice driving with the heater turned up over and over again in a short period of time, it is not feasible to do the same for aerobic exercise, because your body does need to rest.

Give the time intervals between practices some thought. This will take planning, especially if you have a busy schedule. For this reason, it might take 2 weeks or longer to go through all activities on your hierarchy. It is important to practice regularly. Do not put it off!

Given the practical timing issues, it may make sense to work on two activities at one time. For example, you could exercise every second or third day, building up your fitness level, while at the same time practicing getting used to steamy showers. However, with any activity, the practices should be continued until they produce little or no anxiety (2 or less on the 8-point scale).

There is a difference between the sensation-induction exercises done before (e.g., hyperventilating and spinning) and some of the natural activities that you will do over the next few weeks. With sensation-induction exercises, it is clear that the sensations come on quickly after starting the exercise and that they subside quickly after it ends. On the other hand, the onset and end of sensations is less clear with natural activities. The important point to keep in mind is that not knowing exactly when sensations will come and go does not mean you are in more danger. It just means that some activities are not as predictable as the sensation-induction exercises are in terms of bringing on the sensations. The activities may lead to more anticipatory anxiety because of your expectations. For example, you may worry about drinking a cup of coffee because you expect to feel physical effects. In addition, the sensations might not come on right away because it takes some time for caffeine to have an effect. Also, it is not possible to predict exactly when the effects of caffeine will decrease.

Because the sensations are unpredictable, you may tend to focus on the sensations after ingesting caffeine or working out, anxiously waiting for them to go away. However, this approach implies fear of the sensations. Also, the anxious waiting for sensations to disappear makes them last longer, because you are feeding the anxiety or fear response. For example, if you notice your heart racing after drinking a cup of coffee and then interpret this as a sign of heart failure, then, of course, your heart will continue to race. Your heart continues to race because you are giving yourself fearful information, and one of the effects of being afraid is a racing heart.

It is important to realize that the sensations may occur differently than they do during the earlier sensation-induction exercises but that they are not dangerous. Remember, also, that the goal of this treatment is to reduce your sensitivity to physical sensations, whether they are predictable and controllable or not.

Finally, expect to experience different sensations when you do these activities. Do not hope that you will not feel dizzy or shaky. Expect the sensations and learn to be less fearful of them.

Jill's activities for her first 2 weeks were to attend a fitness class (10 minutes each time), first with a friend and then alone, and to have a shower with the curtain drawn and door closed. Her initial ratings of fear level for each activity were 3, 4, and 5, respectively. Her ratings are shown on her Exposure Exercise Record Form (see Figure 12.2). The first time she joined the fitness class, she experienced a considerable amount of anticipation before the class. However, she practiced slow breathing and reminded herself that although she might feel out of breath, hot, sweaty, and a pounding heart, she was not in danger. At one point in the class, Jill had an urge to stop and escape, but then she realized that by going at her own pace she could tolerate the feelings, so she stayed for the full 10 minutes. It is important to control the feeling of wanting to run away or get to safety. After the first practice, Jill found that it became easier and she stayed for longer periods in the class. She then went to class alone. Her fears in the shower also reduced with practice.

Dealing with Frightening Memories

Another method of overcoming fears is to change the way you think about the worst panic you ever had. Sometimes, the memory of an event can be biased. The bias can serve to maintain the fear. For example, perhaps 10 years ago you were bitten by a dog, and the experience was very scary. Every now and then, the

Exposure Exercise Record

See Figure 10.2 in your workbook.

0	1	2	3	4	5	6	7	8
None		**Mild**		**Moderate**		**Strong**		**Extreme**

Write each exercise you practice. For each trial, rate your anxiety/fear according to the scale above.

Day	Exercise	Trial	Anxiety/Fear
1	10 minutes in fitness class —with friend	1	3
2		2	3
3		3	2
4		4	2
5	—alone	1	4
6		2	4
7		3	3
8		4	2
1	Showering with curtain drawn and door closed	1	5
2		2	4
3		3	3
4		4	2

Copyright © 1994 Graywind Publications, Inc. Mastery of Your Anxiety and Panic

Figure 12.2. **Example of Exposure Exercise Record Form**

memory of the dog comes back to you, and you get scared as you think of it. As a result, it is much more likely that you will worry about encountering dogs in the future. In contrast, if you saw the event, not as terrible, but just as unpleasant, then the event is rarely remembered, and the worry about encountering dogs is much less. An important part of this process is that whenever a past event is given a lot of significance (such as when thought of as horrible), it is more easily recalled. The more frequently a memory is recalled, the stronger it gets. Therefore, if you tend to think of the worst panic that you have ever had as being terrifying, something you never want to go through again, and, in fact, if it scares you just to think about it, then the memory might contribute to an anticipation of future panics. In this case, it is important to "process" that memory and make it a less important element in your consciousness.

Many of our clients became less anxious and less on edge about "the next panic attack" after they learned to understand their past panics rather than just being horrified by them. This effect comes from forcing yourself to think about the experience a number of times in an objective way. The process entails doing a sequential analysis.

First, try to recall the worst panic and, as clearly as you can, to remember the context. This context includes the people, the place, the sounds, the colors, the objects that you can see, and anything else there. Try to imagine the event as clearly as you can by placing yourself in the picture, not as an observer, but as someone in the scene. Try to remember how you felt. Remember the sequence of events. What was the first thing that happened? What was your reaction to that? What was the reaction of the other people? How did you feel? What was the next step? You might, indeed, become quite anxious or fearful as you think about that event, but do not stop. Keep thinking about it. Ask yourself if the following kinds of statements go through your mind as you think about that panic: "I hate to even think about it," "I hope I never experience anything like that again," "I couldn't go through that again," "I'm sure I nearly died," "I was so lucky to survive," and so on. If these or similar kinds of statements characterize the way you feel, then you should use repeated exposure to the memory. Think about the event again, particularly the way you felt. Identify the triggers that began the whole cycle including sensations, thoughts, or general stressors. Once the trigger had occurred and you began to react, what were the reactions that you experienced? What was the first sensation that you noticed? How did you react to it? What thoughts came into your mind? Did you make any overestimations? For example, did you think that you were going to die? Did you have catastrophic thoughts? For example, did you feel that everyone would notice and think you were crazy? What was the next thing that happened? Did you become more frightened? Try to understand the sequence of events and how the sensations and thoughts fed into each other. What did you do? Did you go to a hospital or try to escape or call for help or lie down? How did this add to the fear cycle? Did it prove to you that you were in danger, for example? Now again, try to evaluate how you think about that event overall. Indeed, it might have been surprising,

Professor Gallagher and his controversial technique of simultaneously confronting the fear of heights, snakes, and the dark

and it might have been frightening at the time, but that does not mean that if it happened again you would respond in the same way. Go through the memory once more and continue to do so, asking yourself these questions, until you can think about it without feeling anxious.

Exercise

- Plan the activities that you will practice over the next few weeks. Make sure that you practice everyday (or almost everyday) and that you repeat each activity as needed for the fear to reduce to a level of 2. Remember to design the sequence of practices according to each particular activity. That is, sitting in a hot, stuffy room can be practiced repeatedly without long rest periods, whereas showering or eating certain foods may require longer intervals between practices.

Keep a record of your anxiety or fear levels, using the Exposure Exercise Record Form.

- If you find that your memories of past panics make you fearful, practice thinking about them and asking yourself key questions that will let you understand the sequence of what happened and how the panic developed. Continue to review past panic attacks until you no longer feel distressed by the memory of those events.

Self-Assessment

Answer by circling **T** (True) or **F** (False). Answers are provided in Appendix A.

1. If thinking about my worst panic makes me feel anxious, I should avoid thinking about it. **T   F**

2. I should practice each activity daily in order to get the most benefit, and the number of repetitions is based on the level of anxiety I feel. **T   F**

3. If the sensations continue for a long time, that does not mean that they are any more threatening. It is likely that I am focusing on the sensations and becoming worried by them in a way that is unjustified. **T   F**

4. I should proceed with each activity in my hierarchy starting from the activity associated with the lowest level of anxiety. **T   F**

5. It is not terribly important that I record my level of anxiety or fear on the Exposure Exercise Record as long as I complete the exercise itself. **T   F**

6. The exposure practices should be discontinued if they create too great a level of anxiety or fear or too great an intensity of sensation. **T   F**

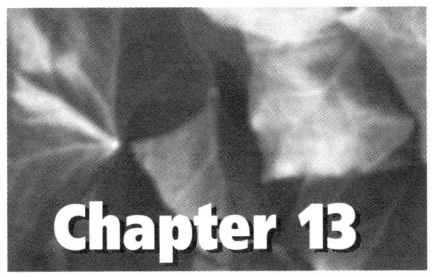

Chapter 13

Overcoming Your Phobic Avoidance: Producing Panic Sensations in Agoraphobic Situations

Review

Review your Daily Mood and Panic Attack Records. Add the information to your Progress Record Form. Did different patterns emerge in the frequency, intensity or sequencing of your panics? Are you are still afraid of having a "panic"? If so, review some of the previous chapters. Fear of panic suggests that there still needs to be some work done on your understanding of what panic is. Go through the three response system analysis. Describe your most recent panic in terms of the sensations, the subjective feelings and thoughts and your behavior. What are the triggers for your fear? What is the first thing that happens? What is your reaction to that and how does it spiral into panic? Also, rate your estimates of probability and ability to cope using your Self-Statement Rating Form. Have your estimates changed? Do you believe the events are less likely to occur or that you are more able to cope with them if they do?

Review your use of self-statement modification and slow-breathing or relaxation strategies. Have you used them when you were uptight or had fearful thoughts? Remember not to use them to escape or fight off the anxiety. They are not designed to prevent fear at all costs. Do not use them to distract you from your feelings. Instead, use them to change the subjective and physical components of your panics.

Review your practices. Did you practice the activities that you had outlined? Did you practice each one enough to feel in control of your emotional response while performing it? Did you practice regularly as opposed to waiting until the last 2 days before returning to this Workbook?

If you have not practiced regularly or if you have not practiced all of the activities that you specified, then continue to do these before going on. You must make these practices a priority. It takes effort, but the more effort you put in the

"It's the mailman, doc. He scares me."

more benefit you will gain. Remember to keep records of your practices on your Exposure Exercise Record Form so you can see how much the anxiety is decreasing with each practice and when to move on to another activity.

Did you try one of your activities, become frightened, and escape the situation? For example, did you sit in a sauna and leave as soon as you felt too hot? If so, then spend some time now thinking about this. What led to your escape? What kind of sensations did you feel? What kind of self-statements were going through your mind? Try to understand why you did not return to the activity. Remember that avoidance serves to confirm your fear and your belief that you cannot cope. Control can only be obtained by overcoming the urge to escape. At first, you may feel a strong wish to leave, but it is essential that you evaluate the basis for that urge. This analysis lets you understand that the urge to escape is based on a misinterpretation of what could happen if you stayed. After identifying the negative thought, you can challenge it with evidence and continue the practice to obtain further evidence of your safety.

Remember that these practices are not supposed to be associated with zero anxiety or fear. You should feel afraid at first, or else there would be no need to do them at all. However, with repeated practice, the fear will decrease. If you did escape, then evaluate your response of escape and return to the activity. Repeat this until you feel comfortable while doing the activity. Then you can make the activity more intense. For instance, if your practice was jogging for 10 minutes, and you feel comfortable with that now, then jog for 20 minutes. If you feel that you have done the activities correctly, then continue with this chapter.

Conquering Agoraphobia—Back to the Shopping Mall

In the first chapter, we discussed phobia or the tendency to avoid places or situations because of fear or panic when no real danger exists. People with panic attacks often avoid, at least to some degree, places or situations where escape might be difficult in the event of a panic attack. The shopping mall is the typical example, but a list of others is presented in Table 13.1. This behavior is called agoraphobic avoidance, and it can last even after you have mastered your panic attacks. There may be some situations that you have avoided, escaped from or endured with fear. These situations may not directly produce sensations, unlike exercise and other activities in the previous chapter. Agoraphobic situations bring on anxiety and panic due to the anticipation of panicking in them.

Typical Agoraphobic-Avoided Situations

- Shopping malls
- Driving
- Car passenger
- Bus passenger
- Trains
- Subways
- Wide streets
- Tunnels
- Restaurants
- Theaters
- Being a long way from home
- Staying at home alone
- Waiting in lines
- Supermarkets
- Stores
- Crowds
- Planes
- Elevators
- Escalators

This chapter outlines briefly how to overcome avoidance. A step-by-step program for this treatment is presented in the Agoraphobia Supplement to this Workbook. In our view, it is important to learn to be less fearful of panic feelings (as you have been doing with this Workbook) before overcoming agoraphobic behaviors. However, if your travel and activities are restricted because of agoraphobic tendencies, now is the time to change that behavior using the methods summarized here and detailed in the Agoraphobia Supplement.

Summary of Steps for Overcoming Agoraphobic Avoidance

The first step is to develop a list of situations that you fear and avoid, placing them in order from least to most difficult.

The situations must be specified as much as possible. For example, driving on a road may not be sufficient if only some roads are feared and avoided. Similarly, fear of shopping may depend on the time of day, whether or not you are alone, and so on. Being specific is important so you can design practices that best fit your needs. Otherwise, the purpose of the practice is lost: practicing driving will not be helpful if you practice only on roads that do not frighten you. Figure 13.1 provides an example of Jill's feared situations:

Next, these situations should be approached repeatedly, with the aid of
(a) rehearsing them in your mind before going into the situation and
(b) trying to bring on the sensations that have been associated with panic while in those situations.

In terms of the way these situations are approached, extensive research suggests that it is effective to proceed gradually. That means starting with the items that are least distressing and gradually working down the list. You can break down each item from the list into different steps. This is the way we have approached the other tasks in this Workbook. For example, shopping for one-half hour alone may begin with shopping for 10 minutes with someone and building to 30 minutes alone. This is the approach we recommend, especially if you are doing this largely on your own.

On the other hand, another way is to "take the bull by the horns," and start with the most difficult item. This means that a lot of fear will be felt at first—It takes a lot of motivation. However, this way is often faster. This is a decision for you to make. Either way, a lot of planning is needed, and it is essential that you follow through with your plan. For this reason, it can help to have someone supervise or prompt you.

Although you may often go into frightening situations, doing so has obviously not worked therapeutically to reduce your fear. If it had, you would not be looking for this kind of treatment. That fact highlights the need to do this kind of practice in a controlled and structured way.

To structure your practice and to maintain your focus, it helps to rehearse the situation in your mind. This rehearsal includes your experiencing of intense sensations and thinking escape-oriented thoughts. Also included is your use of

Specification of Situation-Exposure Tasks

See Figure 13.1 in your workbook.

List situations you fear and avoid
in order from least difficult to most difficult.

1. Shopping in a crowded supermarket for 30 minutes alone
2. Walking five blocks away from home alone
3. Driving on a busy highway for five miles with husband, and alone
4. Eating in a restaurant, seated in the middle
5. Watching a movie while seated in the middle of the row
6.
7.
8.
9.
10.

Copyright © 1994 Graywind Publications, Inc.   Mastery of Your Anxiety and Panic

Figure 13.1.   **Example of Agoraphobic-Avoided Situations**

strategies that control your fear. It is most effective to imagine being frightened and then to imagine staying in the situation and controlling the fear. This rehearsal prepares you for the actual experience.

Related is the importance of accepting and even exaggerating the sensations during the practice. The exposure is not as effective if you try to minimize the sensations. Instead, it is more effective to try to feel dizzy or lightheaded in the shopping mall, for example. This involves a different approach to the sensations. Entering a situation with the intention of having intense sensations is evidence that you do not fear them. If this does not make a lot of sense to you, you might reread some of the earlier chapters. You should be at the point right now of really going for it.

For each practice, records of progress are kept on the Exposure Exercise Record Form. Each situation should be practiced until you can enter the situation without feeling out of control. That is, practice until your anxiety or fear reaches a 2 rating or less. Again, spacing of practices will depend largely on practical concerns. Driving may be easier to repeat quickly than staying home alone. However, if repetitions are done within one practice session, for example, in one afternoon, we recommend you limit them to no more than three. If your fear level is still greater than 2 after three times in one day, start again the next day. It is important that you schedule your practices. Do not wait—Start today. The amount of practice and the number of situations practiced will differ from one person to the next. For that reason, we do not recommend time intervals. However, it would be helpful for you to reread this section of the Workbook at least once per week to remind you of how to do the practices and maintain your focus. Do not stop your progress at this point. Keep working at it if you want to reap the benefits.

It often helps to have the aid of someone when practicing. If you do have a helper, make sure that they have a clear understanding of the purpose of your practices. Also make sure to describe the nature of your anxiety and fear. A helper's presence is useful for two reasons:

- As a way of doing your practices more gradually, if that is the approach you have chosen. For example, if you have difficulty shopping in a crowded mall, it may be easier if you practice with someone. Of course, you must then practice alone so that you learn that you are safe when alone.
- As a way of having a coach to help you use your strategies. That is, your aide can remind you to use breathing control or relaxation she or he notices breathing irregularity or tension. In addition, at regular intervals, your aide can remind you to challenge your self-statements.

For both reasons, it is important that you and your aide are clear on the role of each person. The last thing you want is to get into an argument because you feel pressured by your aide when you are in the shopping mall. Similarly, it would be defeating the purpose of having the aide if you become angry when your aide tries to prompt your use of strategies.

Exercise

The first practical thing to do is to decide if you will benefit from the Agoraphobia Supplement. We recommend the supplement if your life is restricted by agoraphobic fears, for example, if you hesitate to travel more than 10 miles from home, if you wait until other people can go with you to go shopping, or if you avoid long lines. If you fear and avoid very few situations, (e.g., perhaps you have some difficulty with long distance travel only), but your life is not restricted, then the supplement might not be warranted. Instead, you can follow the general principles in this chapter for the few situations that are difficult.

Self-Assessment

Answer by circling **T** (True) or **F** (False). Answers are provided in Appendix A.

1. It is essential that you do not even think about your feelings when you go into different situations. **T F**

2. You may practice confronting situations in either a gradual or an intense fashion, but the most important aspect is to do your practices in a very structured and controlled manner. **T F**

3. Practice each situation once only. **T F**

4. Experiencing anxiety or fear when you are in the situation means you have failed. **T F**

5. Practices must be done regularly. **T F**

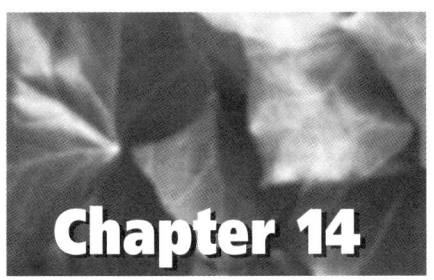

Chapter 14

Medication Issues

Review

Review your Daily Mood and Panic Attack Records. Add the average daily anxiety and number of panic attacks per week to your Progress Record Form. What changes can you see? What about your use of breathing control or relaxation? Did you apply those strategies when you noticed physical sensations or anxiety? Have you had any panics that at first seemed to be unexpected? What triggers could you find? Have you continued to correct overestimations and decatastrophize? What about your ratings on your Self-Statement Rating Form? Are you becoming more confident in your ability to cope or less expectant of negative things happening?

Medications in the Treatment of Panic and Anxiety

Many people with anxiety and panic attacks have had doctors prescribe medication. If this is true for you, you may take this medication regularly or perhaps only when you feel you need it. Many people go through this program without ever starting medication; others would just as soon not take the medication but are doing so on the advice of their physicians. However, there are a number of people who want medication for their anxiety or panic attacks. For some, the anxiety and panic are so severe that they feel they cannot tolerate even one more day and need relief as soon as possible. Even the drug that takes the longest to act would begin to take effect in 3 weeks. Some of the shorter acting drugs can work within a day or two. There is no question that these effects are quicker than the time it takes to complete the program in this Workbook, unless you can spend a lot of time on it and work quickly. Others may not feel that they have the time to devote to mastering the information in this Workbook. Still others may believe strongly that medication is the best treatment for their anxiety.

In any case, as we mentioned in the first chapter, almost 75% of the people who come to our clinic for psychological treatment are taking some kind of medication for their anxiety. Some have been taking it for quite some time. Others were prescribed medication to get them through a few weeks but told to come to our clinic as soon as possible.

As we mentioned before, we do not recommend that these people stop taking their medication before starting the program. Eventually, many people stop on their own. About half of the people completing this program stop taking drugs by the time they finish this program, and others stop sometime during the first year after finishing. Here, we describe ways to use this program to help you stop taking drugs if you want to.

At this point, the evidence seems clear that some types of drugs, if prescribed at the right dosage, can be effective for at least the short-term relief of anxiety or panic for some people. Many of these drugs, however, are not effective in the long term unless you continue to take them. Even then, they may lose some of their effectiveness unless you learn some new, easier method of coping with your anxiety and panic while you are on the drug. Nevertheless, there are some people who begin a course of drug therapy and stop several months later without any need to go through a program such as this. Whether the particular stress they were under has been resolved or whether there were some changes in their sensitivity or whether they developed a different attitude toward their anxiety and panic, this is the only treatment they needed.

For all of these reasons, it seems useful to review briefly the types of medications prescribed for anxiety and panic.

Low-Potency Benzodiazepines (Minor Tranquilizers)

By far, the drugs most commonly prescribed for anxiety and panic are the minor tranquilizers. Two of the most common are diazepam (Valium®) and chlordiazepoxide (Librium®).

Typically these drugs are prescribed for short-term relief of anxiety. They are generally believed to be ineffective for panic attacks unless they are prescribed in very high dosages with which your physician may not feel comfortable. For example, you might need 30 mg or more of Valium® a day to have an effect on your panic attacks. At this dosage, chances are you would feel very sedated. For this reason, minor tranquilizers are seldom prescribed for panic attacks by psychiatrists knowledgeable in the drug treatment of panic. Unless you work carefully with your physician, there is a danger that you may become psychologically and physically dependent on the drug, which is intended only for short-term treatment of anxiety. A new type of antianxiety drug that is not a benzodiazepine is called Buspar® (buspirone). However, this drug does not seem to be effective for panic disorder.

High-Potency Benzodiazepines

In contrast to the low-potency benzodiazepines, high-potency benzodiazepines, such as alprazolam (Xanax®) and clonazepam (Klonopin®), are generally less sedating. These drugs have been shown to be effective in reducing panic attacks in the majority of patients who take them. To give you an idea of how strong Xanax® is, 1 mg of Xanax® equals approximately 10 mg of Valium®. The dose of Xanax® required to block panic attacks varies from person to person and also with the nature of the attacks. Generally speaking, 2–4 mg per day will block spontaneous or unexpected attacks, whereas 4–6 mg per day are required to block situational attacks and to reduce agoraphobic avoidance. Doses up to 10 mg per day are approved by the Food and Drug Administration for the treatment of panic disorder in individuals who need that much. Taking 10 mg of Xanax® would be approximately equivalent to taking 100 mg of Valium®.

While on these dosages, 60% of a large group of patients were free of panic after 8 weeks. However, it can be difficult for people to stop taking high-potency benzodiazepines once they have started. This difficulty occurs because stopping can lead to a quick recurrence of the anxiety or some withdrawal effects of the drug or a combination of both.

These effects can be unpleasant, especially if the drug is tapered too quickly. Under those conditions, many patients report experiencing anxiety and panic even more intensely than they did before starting treatment, a phenomenon known as "rebound." To minimize withdrawal symptoms and rebound, it is important that benzodiazepines be tapered slowly under the close supervision of a doctor, preferably a psychiatrist. Even then, approximately half of the patients will relapse within 6 months of drug discontinuation if they have not had cognitive or behavioral treatment for their panic.

Also, Xanax® has a short half-life, meaning that its effects wear off relatively quickly, generally after 4–8 hours depending on the dosage. As a result, persons taking Xanax® sometimes complain of a return of anxiety between doses, when the medication is wearing off. To avoid that, Xanax® is often prescribed to be taken in three or four doses during the day, usually with meals and at bedtime. Klonopin® has a longer half-life and is usually taken in two or three doses during the day.

Antidepressants

There are three types of antidepressants that seem effective for anxiety and panic attacks. The first type is the tricyclic antidepressants, such as imipramine (Tofranil®) and amytriptyline (Elavil®). Tofranil is, by far, the most commonly used antidepressant for anxiety and panic. A second type of antidepressant drug is the monoamine oxidase inhibitors (MAO inhibitors). The best known drug in this category for anxiety and panic is phenelzine (Nardil®). These two types of drugs seem about equally effective for panic attacks and for avoidance, particularly when combined with the type of program in this Workbook. The major difficulty with these drugs is that during the first 2 or 3 weeks, it is common to have side effects that seem to some people to be similar to anxiety. For that reason, many people do not want to continue taking the drug or at least do not want to increase the dosage to correct levels. However, research has shown that it is important to take enough of this drug to get the full benefits. For example, most people should be taking at least 150 mg of Tofranil® per day to get the most benefit. This dosage will vary somewhat and depends on your physician's judgment. Therefore, if at all possible, one should persist through the first few weeks of taking this drug until reaching that therapeutic dosage.

The MAO inhibitors are used less often for panic attacks because there are severe dietary restrictions when taking this drug. For example, you cannot eat cheese, chocolate, or other foods containing tyramine or drink red wine or beer. If you do, you risk dangerous symptoms including high blood pressure. If you do not mind avoiding these foods and beverages, then you should be taking over 50 mg. a day of the most popular drug, Nardil®, to get the full therapeutic benefit.

It is generally easier for patients to stop taking tricyclic antidepressants than benzodiazepines, partly because the effects of the tricyclics are longer lasting and their withdrawal symptoms are much milder. Probably as a result, relapse rates after discontinuation of antidepressants have generally been found to be lower (perhaps as low as 30%) than those after discontinuation of benzodiazepines. Antidepressants seem most effective when combined with a program such as this one.

A third type of antidepressant is a relatively new class of drugs called selective serotonin reuptake inhibitors (SSRIs). Examples of drugs in this class are fluoxetine (Prozac®) and sertraline (Zoloft®). These drugs are just beginning to be prescribed for panic disorder. They appear to be as effective as the other classes of antidepressants. Some advantages of the SSRIs over the tricyclic antidepressants are that they are less toxic and have fewer side effects. However, like the other antidepressants, they can cause feelings of jitteriness and restlessness and a worsening of panic anxiety when they are first started. To avoid these effects, it is often necessary to start with very low doses, and even then, many patients still have difficulty tolerating these drugs.

Beta Blockers

Many people take beta blockers to reduce blood pressure or regulate heart rate. These drugs act on a specific receptor, the beta receptor, which is involved in physiological arousal. Therefore, if one needs to avoid arousal for medication reasons, beta blockers are often used. Again, there are many types of beta blockers, but the most popular is propranolol (Inderal®). One would think that any medication reducing frightening sensations would have some effect on panic attacks. However, there is little if any evidence that Inderal is useful in any way for panic attacks, although sometimes people feel a bit better. For that reason, doctors knowledgeable about the drug treatment of anxiety rarely prescribe this drug to treat anxiety and panic.

Stopping Your Medication

Now that you have finished this program, you should be ready to stop medication if you wish. If this is a particularly difficult problem for you, an additional brief program for stopping drugs with proven effectiveness is available from The Psychological Corporation to assist you and your doctor. Be very sure that you stop your medication under the supervision of your physician; only he or she can decide how quickly it will be safe for you to taper your medication to the point where you stop it altogether. This approach will be particularly true for drugs like Xanax®, which are best tapered slowly. With what you have learned from this program, you should be able to stop your medication if you follow these guidelines:

- Withdraw from your medication relatively slowly. Do not try to do so all at once. Your physician will be able to give you the best advice on how fast is best for you.

- Set a target date for stopping your medication. Once again, this date will have to be planned with your physician, so make it a reasonable date in view of your own tapering schedule. On the other hand, the date should not be too far away. Generally, the quicker the better as long as it is within a schedule that is safe for you as determined by your physician.

- Use the principles and coping skills that you have learned in this Workbook as you withdraw from the medication.

The reason that we have not addressed this topic until now is because it is important for you to learn how to master your anxiety and panic before successfully stopping medication. One reason for this is that you may begin to experience anxiety and panic at more intense levels as you taper the medication. If you were never on medication, you should be well on your way to mastering panic and anxiety by now. If you are on medication, the principles you have learned will need to be applied again to deal with some increased anxiety and panic as you taper medication. Once again, most people do not find this a problem and gradually reduce their medication as they become more comfortable in dealing with their anxiety and panic.

Most people do not experience increased panic when they taper their medication in this way. If your anxiety seems to be increasing as you reduce your drug dose, it is most likely due to mild withdrawal symptoms. In that case, the symptoms should last only a week or two (in rare cases a little longer) until the drug clears from your system. In addition, you now have the skills to handle this anxiety.

In fact, withdrawal from medication can be seen as the last item on your list of activities described in Chapters 11 and 12. For some reason, withdrawing from medication is another way to produce panic sensations. Therefore, medication withdrawal is an opportunity to apply your strategies for reducing fear and anxiety. Rather than becoming distressed at sensations that come on as you withdraw from drugs, you should follow the guidelines in Chapters 11 and 12 and focus on these sensations until the anxiety is reduced. Of course, you can continue to use your breathing control or relaxation training along with your cognitive strategies.

In other words, treat withdrawal from medication as a final opportunity to develop mastery over your emotions and to eliminate, once and for all, the terrifying feelings of panic. The rewards will be worth it.

Exercise

If you are on medication and wish to withdraw, then your assignment for this week is to speak with your prescribing physician about the best way to do so. Also, plan how you will deal with any of the withdrawal effects by using the various strategies. Draw up a specific step-by-step plan for yourself.

Self-Assessment

Answer by circling **T** (True) or **F** (False). Answers are provided in Appendix A.

1. It is essential that withdrawal from medication is conducted gradually, under the supervision of your prescribing physician. **T F**

2. You are unlikely to feel any different when you withdraw from your medication. **T F**

3. Use any symptoms and anxiety or panic that you experience when withdrawing from medication as an opportunity to apply relaxation, breathing-control, self-statement strategies and exposure principles. **T F**

4. Experiencing physical symptoms or anxiety or panic when withdrawing from medication is a sign of loss of all of your treatment gains. **T F**

5. Experiencing physical symptoms or anxiety/panic when withdrawing from medication is a sign that you will not be able to get off the medication.   T   F

6. The great majority of patients who have completed this program are successfully able to get off panic medications.   T   F

Chapter 15

Your Accomplishments and Your Future

Several issues need to be addressed in this final chapter:

- Examining the changes that you have made since you first began this program
- Determining what the next step is
- Considering methods of maintaining your progress
- Considering high-risk situations for the future, how to deal with your reactions, and which strategies to use

Self-Evaluation

It is time to consider the kind of changes that you have made since you first began this program. This can be done in several ways. An objective method is to look at the Daily Anxiety and Panic Attack Records that you kept. Using your Progress Record Form, examine the changes. First, compare the frequency from the beginning to this point and examine the course of change throughout the program. There may, indeed, be ups and downs. If the frequency or intensity of your episodes of panic and anxiety have decreased, check "yes" in the box next to the item labeled "Panic and Anxiety" on the Self-Evaluation Form in your packet (see Figure 15.1).

Second, look at your Self-Statement Rating Form. Examine the changes in your estimates of the probability and your ability to cope. If you think that you have had a significant reduction in your estimate of the probability and significant increases in your perceived ability to cope with either or both of those items, check the "yes" box next to the item labeled "Self-Statements."

Third, look at your initial ratings of fear in response to the sensation-induction exercises on your Sensation-Induction Record. Now, next to those items, rate your

Self-Evaluation

See Figure 15.1 in your workbook.

Complete this form based on the kinds of changes you have made since you began this program.

	Yes	No
Panic and anxiety Significant reduction in frequency and/or intensity of panic and anxiety episodes	☐	☐
Self-statements Significant reduction in estimates of probability and/or increase in perceived ability to cope with most distressing events	☐	☐
Sensation producing exercises Significant reduction in fear of sensation induction exercises	☐	☐
Activities Significant reduction in fear and/or avoidance of activities associated with panic symptoms	☐	☐

Copyright © 1994 Graywind Publications, Inc.   Mastery of Your Anxiety and Panic

Figure 15.1.   Self-Evaluation Form

current level of fear of those items, using the 8-point scale. If there has been a significant reduction in the fear you associate with these items, check the "yes" box next to the item labeled "Sensation Producing Exercises."

Fourth, on your Activities Hierarchy Form, look at the activities that you associated with fear or avoidance or both because of the sensations they produced. Now, go back and rate your level of fear and avoidance of each activity using the 8-point scale, where 0 means no fear or avoidance, and 8 means extreme fear or avoidance. If you experienced a significant reduction in your fear and avoidance of those activities, check the "yes" box next to the item labeled "Activities."

If you have checked the "yes" box for at least three of the four items, you may consider that you have done very well with this program. If, on the other hand, you have checked "no" to three or more items, there is still room for gains to be made.

What To Do Next

Decide whether you have responded well to the program or if you could still benefit. If you fit into the first category, then your strategy should be to identify areas where you still have concerns and to continue in the same way as you have done so far. Review different sections of the Workbook to help you to deal with areas of difficulty.

If you decide that there is still a lot of room for change, then it is important at this point to try to evaluate possible reasons for that result. There are several possible reasons:

- The initial series of decisions concerning the appropriateness of this program might not have been accurate. In this case, discussion with your doctor or mental health professional should center on further assessment.

- The program takes more time for some people. Taking longer is not necessarily a sign of the lack of success of the program but simply shows a need for continued use of the strategies. If so, continue in the way that you have begun, assuming that there has been some change from the beginning of the program until now. If there has been no progress, then the first possibility listed may be more accurate.

- The program is appropriate, but you have not put in enough effort. This is the most common reason. Have you practiced regularly? Have other events, such as marital problems, taken your attention away? If so, success just depends on renewed effort. If motivation is a more general issue, then it may be better to put the program aside until a time when you are feeling more motivated.

- The fourth possibility is that you have not fully integrated the principles of the program, such as the definition of panic. If this is the case, then a review of all the principles, preferably with your doctor or mental health professional, should help.

Maintenance Planning

If you have done well with this program or are still in the process of achieving control by using the strategies, then one issue to keep in mind is the maintenance of your results. Sometimes people ask, "Will I always be anxious?" and "Does using these strategies simply mean that I'm suppressing an underlying anxiety that is always going to be there?"

In response to the first question, it is important to note that anxiety is normal; everyone experiences anxiety. It would not be helpful to remove anxiety from our lives because it plays such a big role in motivation for performance. We talked about this in the first chapter. Learning to control excessive levels of anxiety is like any other learned behavior; once it is learned, it will probably become more powerful with time and, therefore, more resistant to change.

In response to the second question, it is important to note that this program is not meant to suppress underlying anxiety. Rather, the methods that you have been taught are meant to change the quality of your experiences so that you no longer have excessive anxiety or fear. You are learning to reach the core of your anxiety and fear reactions and to change them. The emotion will always be present because, as mentioned before, anxiety is natural. What you have learned up to this point is to control the unproductive expression of that emotion. You have learned this control in response to certain elements, such as sensations, activities, or situations that are not dangerous and, therefore, do not warrant that emotion. In other words, you have gained control of your emotion.

There are key factors to help you maintain the progress you have made so far. First, whenever you notice yourself hesitating to enter the types of situations or to perform the types of activities described in this Workbook for reasons of fear, that should be a sign for you to go ahead and do it. Do not allow your emotions to direct your behavior. Second, make a point of trying to experience to the fullest all of the sensations that have been associated with your panic in the past. In other words, do things that bring on the sensations and keep reinforcing your sense of control. Third, whenever you do experience anxiety or fear, remember to use the objective analysis you used here. Rather than being overwhelmed by your fear, evaluate the triggers, sequencing ,or interactions. Only in cases where there is a real danger, such as an oncoming car, should your fear be considered a rational response that need not be questioned.

In general, it will help at times to reread different parts of the Workbook. If you have a panic attack in the future, do not treat that as a relapse or a sign that you have lost all that you have gained. That is a time when you must apply, to the fullest extent, an approach of objective understanding. Try to analyze the reasons for the fear using your strategies. Indeed, you may expect that at some time in the future, you will become frightened again. Try not to hope that you will never feel that way again. If you say this to yourself, then it is a sign that you have not learned to understand fear differently.

High-Risk Times

From our work, it has been shown that the likelihood of becoming fearful again is increased at times of stress. It seems that the stress affects the central nervous system in a way that makes the person generally more aroused or tense as we described in earlier chapters. Therefore, you are more likely to experience sensations. The important thing to realize is that if you do become frightened by the sensations, there are probably some unproductive interactions going on between your interpretations and your feelings. That is, experiencing stress and its effects does not mean you must feel anxiety and panic. Anxiety and panic only develop when you respond to that stress and its effects fearfully. That response is under your control.

Finally, congratulations on finishing this program! You have worked hard to get to this point and you deserve all of the credit in the world for the work that you have done. We sincerely hope that you are well on your way to regaining control over your life and that you have escaped from the grasp of your negative emotions. Perhaps you are there already. If so, then we hope that you are under the influence of another emotion—You can feel this one in the form of satisfaction with your success.

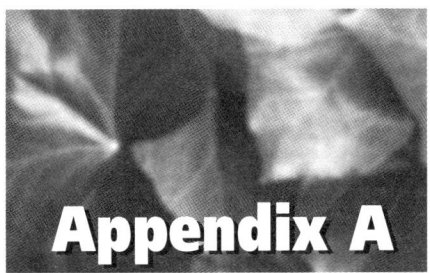

Appendix A

Answers for Self-Assessment Questions

Chapter 1

1. **True.** Many people have occasional panic attacks without developing panic disorder. In order for a person to meet the criteria for the diagnosis of panic disorder, he or she has to experience apprehension about the possibility of a future panic attack. People who have had a panic attack but who do not worry about having another attack would not meet the criteria for the diagnosis of panic disorder.

2. **True.** In addition to the unpleasant physical sensations, people often report having thoughts of going crazy, losing control, or dying while they are having a panic attack.

3. **False.** Panic attacks and agoraphobia are very common problems. From 3% to 6% of the population are estimated to experience agoraphobia. This means that approximately 7–12 million people in the United States alone have agoraphobia.

4. **False.** Distraction may be useful in the short term to help people get through a fearful situation, but, in the long run, it is not helpful because it does not allow for new learning to take place and to alter the underlying processes that lead to panic attacks.

Chapter 2

1. **True.** Monitoring is an essential component of the development of control over anxiety and fear because it provides the basis from which to understand your emotions and to implement appropriate strategies.

2. **False.** Avoiding thinking about your feelings is understandable when the feelings are distressing, but avoidance does not allow one to learn

the core elements of different emotional reactions, knowledge that is a necessary ingredient for learning to control such reactions.

3. **False.** It is most effective to monitor panic attacks as soon as possible after their occurrence because recall tends to be biased and inaccurate.

4. **True.** Using monitoring techniques, one is able to determine the situations in which panic occurs most often and the factors that are most likely to precipitate panic. Identification of those factors is important to the development of a sense of control, because it heightens awareness of the fact that panic and anxiety are reactions rather than uncontrollable events.

5. **True.** Your levels of anxiety and depression and anticipation of panic can be recorded at the end of the day, by taking an overview of the day and calculating averages.

Chapter 3

1. **True.** The basic components of anxiety and fear are physiology, thoughts, and behaviors, and it is the interaction among those three components that determines the intensity of the emotional responses of anxiety and fear.

2. **False.** Anxiety is a natural human emotion that everyone experiences and is indeed often a productive driving force. The goal of this program is to reduce levels of anxiety that are excessive and pervasive.

3. **True.** It is essential that you understand the interactions among physical sensations, interpretations, and behaviors. By definition, panic includes physiological arousal and subjective fear. Hence, if there was no fear of the sensations, there would be no panic.

4. **False.** Hereditary factors seem to play some role in determining level of general sensitivity that may predispose some individuals to the development of anxiety, but heredity does not explain all of panic.

5. **True.** Anxiety and panic are different emotions. The hallmark of panic is a sudden rush of fear with focus on the immediate present, whereas anxiety is usually anticipatory in nature.

6. **True.** Anxiety and fear are composed of thoughts, physical feelings, and behaviors. Therefore, the treatment program presented in this Workbook targets these three components of anxiety and fear by teaching you to alter your panic responses by learning to change the way you think and the way you react physically and behaviorally.

Chapter 4

1. **False.** Although medical factors may be involved in panic attacks, a panic attack is not solely a medical problem over which you have no control. Panic is a reaction of fear to something, whether that something be a belief of being in danger or intense physiological arousal.

2. **False.** The symptoms experienced during panic, such as a racing heart and sweating, are natural sensations associated with arousal of the autonomic nervous system that occur during episodes of fear. The physical symptoms reflect activation of a biological mechanism, which is, in fact, designed for the protection of the organism.

3. **True.** Panic is a fight-or-flight reaction designed to protect the organism from danger. In panic disorder, panic attacks occur in the absence of real danger.

4. **True.** Although panics may seem unpredictable, they can always be tied to a cue or signal. Sometimes those cues are very subtle, such as fluctuations in breathing rate or intense emotion unrelated to fear, and, therefore, the experience of panic seems to be unpredictable.

5. **False.** The body's central nervous system has a built in inhibitor that counteracts activation of the sympathetic nervous system. Anticipatory anxiety may produce symptoms over long periods of time, but the actual panic attack is a relatively short event.

6. **True.** Going crazy is not a consequence of panicking. The worst that can happen during a panic attack is intense distress.

Chapter 5

1.a. **True.** Overbreathing refers to excessive inhalation of oxygen and a proportionate reduction in the level of carbon dioxide in the blood. If the body uses up oxygen at the rate at which it is inhaled, a state of overbreathing does not occur.

1.b. **False.** Continuous overbreathing may result in fainting. Fainting is a useful bodily response, during which time a balance between oxygen and carbon dioxide in the blood is reestablished.

1.c. **False.** During breathing retraining exercises, it is important to focus on counting and the word relax. The attention component to the exercise is important for learning to control patterns of fear and anxiety.

1.d. **False.** Speeding up of the breathing rate during breathing retraining exercises is an indication of the need to continue to practice and is probably a result of fearful hypersensitivity to breathing symptoms.

1.e. **True.** Breathing retraining is used as a technique to eliminate the symptoms that have become signals for panicking and to reduce the level of physiological arousal that occurs during panic attacks.

2.a. **False.** Physical tension can occur both acutely and chronically, but the long-term presence of tension does not imply an inability to achieve relaxed states.

2.b. **True.** Experiencing excessive levels of muscular tension can worsen subjective feelings of anxious anticipation and fear.

2.c. **True.** A high level of muscular tension can produce fatigue, muscle aches, pains, and weakness because of the excessive amount of energy used.

2.d. **False.** Learning to relax is achieved through progressive steps, the first of which is learning to relax the body very gradually by focusing on different muscle groups.

2.e. **True.** Relaxation methods are designed to eliminate the symptoms that have become cues to which the person is hypersensitive and to reduce the level of physical tension that occurs during panic.

3. **False.** From 50% to 60% of people who panic overbreathe. This fact underscores the significance of breathing retraining in the treatment of panic disorder.

4. **False.** Learning muscle relaxation can produce fear in two ways. First, fear of relaxation can occur because of the sense of losing control. Relaxation involves letting one's guard down or giving up some control, and this can be anxiety provoking for people who fear harmful or dangerous things at all times. Second, relaxation can trigger fear because some of the physical sensations it can produce, for example, floating feeling, may be associated with panics you have had in the past. In either case, feeling fearful is not a reason to discontinue muscle relaxation. In fact, just the opposite is true. Feeling fearful is all the more reason to learn muscle relaxation because the primary method of getting over increased sensitivity to sensations of fear is repeated, controlled exposure.

Chapter 6

1. **True.** Skipping out on practices once in a while is okay, but it is essential that, overall, practices be conducted regularly. The amount of effort that is put into practicing determines the amount of benefit that is gained.

2. **True.** Focusing on the techniques of breathing retraining or relaxation is essential to the effectiveness of these procedures. Learning to control emotional reactions entails a shifting of focus of attention away from sensations and feelings of being out of control to methods of being in control.

3. **False.** That it takes time to attain benefit from breathing retraining or relaxation is not an indication that those techniques will never work.

4. **True.** Monitoring of exercises using relaxation or breathing retraining is very important for several reasons, including an awareness of their effectiveness and understanding reasons for which they were implemented more or less successfully.

Chapter 7

1. **False.** Thoughts impact greatly on one's feelings just as one's feelings impact greatly on thoughts. Thinking that danger is imminent will, of course, increase levels of anxiety, and feeling anxious will increase the likelihood of thinking that one is in danger.

2. **True.** The first step in learning to correct anxiety-provoking thoughts or self-statements that are inaccurate is to identify the thoughts or self-statements as clearly and specifically as possible. Only then is one in a position to apply appropriate control techniques of questioning the evidence and decatastrophizing.

3. **False.** The belief that self-statement modification is not effective because "I am still afraid that it could happen" is a contradiction in terms. Stating that you are afraid "it could still happen" indicates that the initial thought concerning danger or threat has not been modified.

4. **True.** Questioning of one's thoughts enables one to interrupt the emotional cycle and to examine the interactions between one's thoughts and feelings.

5. **True.** Fearful negative thoughts do become stronger or more believable during periods of intense anxiety. This is called mood–thought congruency. However, the fact that a negative thought becomes more believ-

able when one is anxious does not mean that the likelihood that the feared event will come true is increased.

6. **True.** Negative thoughts can become so automatic that you may be unaware of their influence on you. This point is important because it is possible for these negative thoughts, of which you are unaware, to lead to increases in anxious physiological arousal that may then trigger a panic. The fact that you may experience physiological arousal in the absence of an immediately identifiable negative thought can contribute to the feeling that your panic has occurred "out of the blue."

Chapter 8

1. **False.** It is easy to confuse the presence of thoughts as an indication of their validity, but simply worrying about events such as fainting or going crazy does not increase the chances of those events actually happening.

2. **False.** Everyone experiences unpleasant or distressing thoughts, but people differ in the frequency with which those thoughts occur.

3. **True.** Despite feeling that it is hard to think rationally at times when you are very anxious or panicky, it is important to continue to evaluate what is going on in an objective manner. Use key questions such as "What am I worried about?" "What are the real odds of that happening?" "So what if it does happen?". Remember, even if you have difficulty thinking rationally, you will not be in any danger because the emotional state will pass.

4. **True.** Forcing yourself to contemplate your worst fears will initially induce more anxiety, but the most effective method of learning control is to face those concerns front on and to learn that they are invalid and inaccurate. By avoiding thinking about the things that frighten you, you are in some ways adding confirmatory evidence to those fearful images or thoughts.

5. **False.** Breathing control is simply a tool to target the physical component of anxiety. It is not meant to be used as a desperate means of preventing a panic attack. In fact, using it as a means of avoiding a panic attack at all costs simply increases your anxiety. Remember, even if you never learn to slow your breathing, your panic symptoms will subside, and you will survive.

6. **False.** Due to the automatic manner in which negative fearful thoughts may occur, it can be quite difficult to learn to identify and alter these thoughts. So, although the general concept of challenging one's beliefs

may be easy to understand, it can be difficult to apply and should be given as much attention as breathing control or muscle relaxation practices.

7. **True.** It is not uncommon for people to believe that panic attacks are unmanageable and will continue forever, especially while they are experiencing one. However, this thinking reflects both overestimating the probability of panics and catastrophizing the outcome of panics. It is important for you to remember that even if you do nothing, a panic attack will pass—Panic attacks are time-limited and manageable.

Chapter 9

1. **True.** Although panic attacks may seem to occur unexpectedly, that is not an indication that the panics occur without reason and are, therefore, uncontrollable. In contrast, panic attacks are reactions, but sometimes the cues that stimulate the onset of panic are very subtle and hard to identify. In those cases, it might seem that the panic is unpredictable.

2. **False.** That a panic attack is seemingly unpredictable or appears to come "from out of the blue" it does not mean that the panic is more threatening. You are in no more danger when you experience a panic while at home alone.

3. **False.** Although the methods of relaxation and breathing retraining are designed to control physical symptoms, failure in applying those techniques will not result in increasing the chance of danger. They are simply management techniques, and even if you are not able to apply those techniques successfully, you will still survive panic.

4. **True.** Panic can be precipitated by a variety of events ranging from external, stressful happenings to subtle, internal events, such as a fluctuation in your heart rate or worrying about future panic attacks or feeling out of breath from running up a flight of stairs.

5. **False.** The goal of self-statement modification is to correct the incorrect thinking that contributes to fear and anxiety. In turn, reduction in fear and anxiety will lessen the physical sensations. However, the reduction in sensations does not always occur right away, and it can take a while for the sensations to dissipate. The important thing to bear in mind is that self-statement modification allows for this dissipation of sensations to occur more quickly than it would if you persisted in thinking the incorrect negative thought.

Chapter 10

1. **True.** An essential component of the therapy procedure is to allow yourself to experience to the fullest degree the elements of which you are afraid. That means experiencing the physical sensations at a very intense level and experiencing the feelings of anxiety fully. Failing to do so might result in a tendency to disconfirm the practices that you have done and to continue to fear that you would not be able to cope when the sensations or the anxiety do become intense.

2. **False.** Despite the general labels of panic disorder or anxiety disorder, there are many individual differences in the way in which anxiety and panic are experienced and the elements to which individuals are most sensitive. For that reason, you must tailor your practices to the elements of which you are most afraid.

3. **True.** Each exercise should be practiced repeatedly until the initial level of anxiety that is experienced is only mild. Remember that when you first begin to practice, you should not prevent the experience of anxiety: It is expected that initial anxiety or fear will be high and then will reduce with repeated practice.

4. **False.** Do not prevent the development of anxiety or fear before the exercise. That is, use the management techniques of thought analysis or breathing retraining or relaxation only after you have gone through the exercises.

Chapter 11

1. **False.** Reexperiencing panic after a period of time without panic is not an indication of relapse or loss of gains made. It simply reflects the need to continue to practice. It is very natural for people to reexperience panics at different times and, in fact, the experience of intense fear is a great opportunity for learning.

2. **True.** At times when the anxiety or fear is intense, it is helpful to identify the most feared event and ask a set of key questions such as "What are the real odds of this happening?" and "So what if it does happen?"

3. **False.** It is important to realize that by attempting to "fight off the feelings of fear at all costs" you are, in fact, not evaluating the reasons for experiencing fear and, therefore, not implementing appropriate methods of control. In addition, fighting off anxiety or fear adds fuel to the experience of anxiety or fear because fighting increases tension.

4. **True.** There is no question that the more practice you perform the more benefit you will gain. This point cannot be emphasized too much.

Chapter 12

1. **False.** Becoming anxious or fearful when recalling your worst panic attacks is an indication of the need to continue to think about those past events until you are able to evaluate them objectively and to be less fearful of the memory. By avoiding thinking about those past events, you are maintaining a fear of their recurrence.

2. **True.** Daily practice is the most effective method of learning to change one's reactions, and the number of repetitions for each activity depends on the level of anxiety experienced. Continue the activity the number of times required until you experience no more than mild levels of anxiety. However, do not practice more than five times in any one session because you will simply exhaust yourself.

3. **True.** The persistence of symptoms over a long period of time does not necessarily indicate that they are dangerous. It is likely that their persistence is based, at least in part, on your continuing attention to those symptoms and worry about them. By anxiously worrying about one's bodily symptoms, you increase general levels of arousal, and the presence of the symptoms is more likely.

4. **True.** It is important that the practices you conduct are carried out in a systematic and controlled manner. Begin with the least difficult items on your hierarchy and work up to the most difficult item.

5. **False.** It is important that you record your level of anxiety or fear on the Exposure Exercise Record Form so that you may track reductions in your fear and anxiety and note your progress. Remember that you should continue practicing a particular exposure exercise until you experience only mild levels of anxiety while doing it.

6. **False.** The purpose for doing the exposure exercises is to experience the sensations and to learn that they are not harmful and need not be feared. Discontinuing exposure practices does not allow corrective learning to take place and defeats the purpose of the practices.

Chapter 13

1. **False.** When you practice different situations that, in the past, you avoided or endured with anxiety or fear, it is important that you remain focused not only on where you are but also on what you feel in those situations. Trying to avoid the way that you feel may, in fact, alleviate the level of anxiety/fear at that moment but does not enable you to learn how to feel differently in the long term.

2. **True.** You can confront the situations that you have been avoiding or enduring with dread by using either a very intense approach or by a very gradual approach. Whatever approach you choose, the most important aspect is to do the practices regularly, systematically, and in a controlled manner. Use your self-monitoring to keep on track.

3. **False.** The number of practices that you conduct for each situation listed on your hierarchy depends on the level of anxiety that you experience. Continue to practice the number of times that is necessary in order to reduce your anxiety to a mild level.

4. **False.** You are, in fact, expected to experience some anxiety or fear when you first practice the situations that you have been avoiding or enduring with dread. The presence of anxiety or fear during your practice is certainly not an indication of failure but an indication that you are facing the most relevant situations.

5. **True.** Practices must be done regularly.

Chapter 14

1. **True.** Discontinuation of your medication should be conducted under the supervision of the physician prescribing your medication because it is possible that you may experience increased anxiety or withdrawal symptoms if your medication is tapered too quickly. Only your doctor can decide how quickly it will be safe for you to taper your medication to the point where you can stop altogether.

2. **False.** Taking medication is a physiological intervention for panic or anxiety that can produce unpleasant panic sensations when it is discontinued. Therefore, it is possible that you may feel different when you discontinue your medication. However, these sensations may be minimized by appropriate tapering of your medication, and they provide an opportunity for you to practice the strategies that you have learned to cope with anxiety or panic.

3. **True.** You should use any withdrawal symptoms and anxiety or panic that you may experience as you taper your medication as an opportunity to apply relaxation, breathing-control, or self-statement strategies and exposure principles. It is helpful to view any symptoms that you may experience while discontinuing your medication as simply another exercise in exposure to unpleasant, fear-producing sensations.

4. **False.** Experiencing physical symptoms or anxiety or panic when withdrawing from medication is not a sign that you have lost all of the gains that you made during treatment. As with other physiological factors such as hyperventilation, withdrawal from medication may, by

itself, produce panic sensations. Therefore, any increased anxiety that you may experience upon medication withdrawal should be viewed as simply another opportunity to apply your newly learned strategies for reducing fear and anxiety.

5. **False.** Experiencing physical symptoms or anxiety or panic when withdrawing from medication is not a sign that you will not be able to get off medication. Medication is a physiological intervention for anxiety or panic that may produce panic sensations when discontinued. However, these withdrawal symptoms typically last only a week or two and may be minimized by appropriate tapering of your medication. The fact remains that most people, whether they experience withdrawal symptoms or not, stop taking drugs by the time they complete this program, and others stop sometime during the first year after finishing.

6. **True.** The majority of patients who have completed this program are successfully able to discontinue panic medications.

References

American Psychiatric Association. (1994). *Diagnostic and statistical manual of mental disorders* (4th ed.). Washington, DC: Author.

Barlow, D. H. (1988). *Anxiety and its disorders: The nature and treatment of anxiety and panic.* New York: Guilford Press.

Beck, A. T., & Emery, G. (1985). *Anxiety disorders and phobias.* New York: Basic Books.

For more information on Graywind Publications or TherapyWorks products, please contact The Psychological Corporation at **1–800–228–0752 (TDD 1–800–723–1318)**.

- C. LOEFFLER -
MAY 77